Creatin[illegible]

Crea[illegible]
Life: The Lessons I
Learned From Yoga
and My Mom

MW01289598

Jennifer Williams-Fields

Creating A Joyful Life

Copyright © 2010 Jennifer Williams-Fields

Edited by Jane Goltz

Original artwork by Rayna Curtin

Cover Art by MJC

Published by Homefolk Media

All rights reserved.

DEDICATION

To the women who came before me, to those who have stood next to me, and to my daughters who are just beginning their path, this is for you.

To my mom, my first teacher, my confidante and my friend, this is for you. I miss you every day.

From small things momma…

TABLE OF CONTENTS

ACKNOWLEDGEMENTS

This book wouldn't be possible without the help of many people. Thank you to the women who not only shared their stories with me but willingly allowed me to share their stories here with you. To everyone who continued to ask me "how's the book coming?" and the special ones who held me accountable when I felt like giving up. Thank you to those who gave me their time, their energy and their help when I needed it.

Although there are too many to name, and I apologize if I leave anyone out, I have to say thank you to Wanda, Diane, Mary, Kate, Kim, Linda, Marissa, Jan, Kerri, Bing, Lindsey, Lisa, Amy, Christy, Margaret and Rayna. You believed in me even when I didn't.

When we first met, I told you Randy I was going to write a book someday. You told me to do it. When I started blogging and remembering my dream to write a book you said do it. When I shared the most difficult parts of this book with you, you said do it. Thank you for never once, not even at the end, saying no, you can't do that. Our story didn't end as planned, but it was one hell of an adventure.

Matt, Dave, John, Abby, Danny and Maggie, you are the reason I do what I do. Thank you for all the times you took care of each other while I was working, for giving me the space I needed when I needed it and for putting up with me writing during all your dance and sports practices. Most of all, thank you for being my kids. You were my strength in my weakest times.

There you go kids. I promised I'd get your name in the book!

Creating A Joyful Life

FOREWARD

No one would wish for anyone the kind of emotional and literal hurricane that Jennifer had to endure in certain seasons of her life but through it and beyond it she makes visible to us that there is a measurable hope and lightness can be obtained with the lessons of yoga and motherhood, insight from her own mother and her code for living soulfully. Brene Brown says, "the moments that made me are the moments where I came out from underneath something I didn't know I could come out from underneath from." These moments of struggle are the ones that shape and form us into who we really are. When we allow it, these defining moments of struggle can ultimately prune us into raw, heart centered humans that enable us to connect to ourselves, our family and to the community at large in a real and lasting way.

This is precisely what Jennifer achieves in her book. There is a growth and depth in the journey she shares with us that gives us a clear mirror into ourselves because we can relate so easily with her odyssey. Each chapter had me reaching in, rummaging around and plucking out another gem of truth within me. I found by the end, I am ever more enriched by her gentle guiding words and powerful story which coaxed me in the direction of wholeness.

Jennifer shows us that when we shelter ourselves from struggle we can become numb to both the trials and the joys. Bit by bit, we can see that her struggles allow us to learn compassion for others and thankfully, ourselves. Sometimes just coming to know that none of us are alone in this wild trek and that we can embrace diverse (code name for crazy) family, our own incredible uniqueness and learn to appreciate how very much the same we are, is lesson enough.

However, she drives us further into ourselves to assist us in overcoming even our darkest fears and "hiding the closet" moments. When we begin to have honest conversations about ourselves on how we can move through, rather than around the fears, we begin to see how we can accept the love in our own worthiness.

Taking the precepts of yoga and the nuggets of wisdom offered by her late mother, Jennifer shows us how to overcome obstacles and march forward with joy into life. We sew together our imperfections, realizing we are already whole. I love that through the reflections she offers, we can begin to see threads of grace and wholeness that bind us all.

May this book bring you as much enrichment into your life as it has mine.

Melissa Smith

Friend and Fellow Sojourner

Melissasmithyoga.com

INTRODUCTION

August 2005: I'm stuck watching time drag by as I sit in traffic headed north just hours before Hurricane Katrina will hit New Orleans. I don't realize it yet, but in just a few hours everything I thought was important will soon be gone forever. Although I should be, I'm not scared. I'm too tired to even care.

As I sit in traffic my thoughts wander from the mundane to the extreme. Did I lock the back door? Why didn't I bring the kids schoolwork or even their social security cards? I had a premonition when I first heard we were moving to New Orleans that it would end badly. But I don't remember ever anticipating this. Each thought leads to the same question. How the hell did I get here?

I'm not just stuck in traffic. I'm stuck in my life.

My marriage is in a state I believe to be beyond repair. I don't even care enough to try to fix it anymore. My journalism career that was going to change the world is long abandoned and forgotten. Everyone keeps telling me I just have postpartum depression. I'm not depressed. I hate my life and I hate who I've become. All I know now is I feel defeated and dejected. I'm tired, I'm lonely and I'm done. I don't even know who I am anymore.

I realize if I can just make it out of this line of cars I can go anywhere. I can leave all the sadness and anger behind. If I just keep driving I can become someone new. I can start a new life.

And then I look in the rearview mirror. Staring back at me are the confused and anxious eyes of six children ranging in age from newborn to ten years old. Sitting between them in the car are a big dog, a bag of dirty laundry, a box of crackers, and assorted odds and ends I threw into the car when the local authorities knocked on my door and said mandatory evacuation.

At this moment piled in the back of the car is all I have in the world. And I have no idea where I'm going or what to do.

January 2011: I'm sitting on my front porch swing on an unusually warm winter day. My face is turned toward the sun, a slight breeze is blowing, and the rhythm of the swing is soothing.

The six little kids are now older. I'm married to the same man. The big dog is now covered in gray fur. There is still dirty laundry, crackers and assorted odds and ends scattered in both my car and my new home.

Nothing has changed, but everything is different. I am content. I am at peace.

I gained a new perspective on the same old things and with that, my life changed. I've changed. I have a new career I feel a calling to. I've started writing again. I'm happier. I'm proud of what I've done and who I've become.

Yet, I have no idea of the new storm that is brewing and about to knock me off my feet. A storm that will challenge everything I've learned, everything I teach and everything I believe.

Some nights I don't know that I'll make it through to the next day and some nights I don't even want to. I will become totally broken. It will take a strength I didn't know I had to just survive.

I don't yet realize that all the self-improvement work I've been doing on myself is to prepare for me the biggest test yet to come.

My story isn't all that different than most women's. I forgot who I was. I lost myself in the responsibilities of marriage and children. By today's reality TV standards my six kids don't even count as a large family. I'm not a celebrity. I don't promise a quick fix or a magic cure.

But I do know the long and, sometimes painful, path I took is available to everyone. I now have the tools I need to remind myself daily not only of who I am, but that I am loved.

The lessons I learned are universal to all women. They are the lessons I learned from yoga and my mom.

ABOUT THIS BOOK

My mom was a yogi before the term yogi went mainstream and became synonymous with expensive yoga pants, yoga teacher trainings and mala beads. A flower child of the Sixties, my mom was raised on 'all you need is love', the laws of karma and female empowerment. As far as I know she never stepped foot onto a yoga mat until I became a yoga teacher and she came to my class just to be sure I had at least one student in attendance.

She did, however, live a yogic life. She believed in the inherent goodness of everyone. She encouraged taking care of both your physical body and your inner spirit. She found joy in the mundane and celebrated life.

This book is an assortment of lessons I learned from my mom and my yoga studies. The messages my twentieth-century mom shared with me are remarkably in tune with the 5,000-year-old teachings of yoga philosophy. As a yoga teacher I speak with my students about taking what we learn during our time spent on the mat and applying those lessons to our real life off the mat. My mom was ahead of her time in living off the mat.

Sanskrit is the ancient language of yoga. Yoga is actually derived from the Sanskrit word yuj, which means to unify or yoke. Yoga strives to unify the body, mind and spirit.

There is a disconnect going on now in the body, mind and spirit of too many women. It doesn't have to be this way. There is a better way to live a truly authentic life.

You don't need to be a yoga student to apply the lessons in this book to your life. In fact, if you've never even considered stepping on a yoga mat, then you'll still be able to relate to the issues facing all women.

Each chapter weaves together an issue women face, a yoga teaching and my mom's advice. At the end of each chapter is a page titled Vikram. A Sanskrit word, Vikram is composed of the roots Vi: meaning to work and kram: a step, stride or path. Vikram embodies the principle of thoughtful and devoted actions.

Some of the Vikram suggestions may speak to you, some may challenge you. Some you might not be comfortable with. It's one thing to read the advice and the lessons other women have encountered. However, change doesn't happen until we apply those lessons. You are reading this book because you are ready for a change.

Change doesn't happen overnight. The first step, however, is being willing to make a change. Be thoughtful, be mindful and be willing to devote your actions to finding a happier, more peaceful you.

You are a strong powerful woman and you come from a lineage of strong powerful women. It's time to harness that power. You are ready.

"No one can save us but ourselves. No one can and no one may. We ourselves must walk the path."

Buddha

Lokah Samastah Sukhino Bhavantu

May all beings everywhere be happy and free, and may the thoughts, words, and actions of my own life contribute in some way to that happiness and to that freedom for all.

1

I'M NOT THE CRAZY ONE. AM I?

My major life change began with a very simple, yet seemingly random thought. I'm not the crazy one!

Am I?

Listen closely. I'm going to tell you something you probably don't want to hear and most likely won't believe. What I'm about to say may go against everything you've been telling yourself for too long.

You are exactly where you are supposed to be.

The choices you've made have been neither good nor bad. They have been the choices made to the best of your ability at the time you made them.

Your life up to this point has happened exactly as it was supposed to. Wherever you live, whomever you live with, whatever your circumstance is, you are exactly where you are supposed to be.

You are not trapped. You are not stuck. You are not defeated. You are in the right place at the right time to embark on a transformation of body and soul.

I know what you're going to say. Your situation is different. You got married too young. You didn't plan on having children. You sure didn't plan on raising a special needs child. You should have finished college or stayed active in your career. You married the wrong guy or you let the right guy get away. The list is long of what you should have done, you never did and you regret doing.

No, you are only stuck for as long as you choose to be stuck. You are here at this moment for a reason. I don't know what your specific reason is, and odds are you don't know either. But the reason is inside you and it is screaming to get out. But first you need to get rid of the guilt, the regret, the bitterness, the resentment and the pain. It no longer serves you. It's not who you are.

It's no coincidence you picked up this book today. Your soul wants to be set free. Deep inside not only do you desire to fly, but you know you are capable of spreading your wings and soaring.

Perhaps you are reading this book standing in the aisle of the bookstore. Or trying to stay awake while lying in bed after another monotonous yet grueling day. Maybe you are standing in the bathroom with the water running praying 'Dear God please just give me five minutes alone.'

Congratulations! Your past has led you to this place right here right now. You have the opportunity to make a new choice, a different choice. A choice to open yourself to abundance and joy and discover who you really are.

I wish I could show you

When you are lonely or in darkness

The astonishing light

Of your own Being!

"I Heard God Laughing" Poems of Hope and Joy

Renderings of Hafiz by Daniel Ladinsky

So how the hell did you get here? Who are you? Can you even begin to answer those questions? Relax. It's ok if you can't. In fact, it's pretty normal.

I was just 18 when I met my future husband and only 20 when I married him. Of course, I was thrilled when he proposed. After all, I had grown up on Disney fairytales. In hindsight though, I was too young to even know what I wanted, who I was or where I was going.

Although I had my parents blessing to get married, my mother pulled me aside and said to me "Don't lose yourself."

Don't lose myself? How could I not eventually lose myself when I didn't even know who I was to begin with?

As so often naturally happens, after the marriage the babies start coming. Pretty soon, like most women, I became bogged down in midnight feedings, laundry, dishes and lack of sleep.

Once sleep deprivation sets in, the mind begins to play games with you. Forgetfulness, moodiness, irritability, lack of joy are all common side effects of not enough sleep. And since most women falsely believe they just need to put on a happy face and suck it up, our inner spirit is spiraling downward so fast we don't even realize it.

We are smiling on the outside and crying on the inside. Is it any wonder we begin to question our own sanity?

And maybe we are crazy if we don't know who we are or what we identify with anymore. How many times have you heard a woman describe herself as "just a mom"? It doesn't matter if she has a masters degree or an exciting career, we women become so attached to caring for our families that we lose sight of the fact that we are human with human needs. We give our all to everyone at the expense of ourselves.

The "just a mom" comment is an example of what in yoga we call negative samskaras. Samskaras are thought patterns that we repeat over and over again until not only do we believe them, but in the case of negative samskaras we become stuck in them.

Think of a record on a turntable. (Those of you too young to know what a turntable is, just bear with me here.) You place the needle on the record and are singing along. Suddenly the record starts to repeat itself on a specific section of the song you don't really like. There is a groove on the record the needle can't get out of. If you don't lift the needle, the repeated sound will become not just annoying but maddening.

I'm just a mom. I'm not qualified anymore for my career. I'm a bad housekeeper. I'm not a good mom like those women are. If I were a good wife I'd be skinnier, cook better meals, and dress sexier.

You've heard it all right? You may have even said a few of these statements yourself. You are lying to yourself. And one of the most dangerous things we can do is believe our own lies.

The Buddha said "what we think, we become." So the more we allow and reinforce negative thinking - those negative samskaras – the more down and out we are going to feel.

Down But Not Out

And once we are down, it's hard to see our way back up. In fact, it can just seem easier to let ourselves keep going down.

Whether you call it the baby blues, feeling in a funk or out of sorts, conservative estimates from the Mayo Clinic cite depression as affecting one in eight women in their lifetime.

Factor in hormonal changes, lifestyle, lack of social support, low self-esteem, sleep deprivation and societal pressure, and more than twice as many women as men will suffer bouts of depression between the ages of 25 and 44 years old.

What else usually happens between the ages of 25 and 44? We get married, start families and build careers. It's a perfect storm that has the power to either catapult us forward or force us down into a deep bottomless pit.

The deep bottomless pit is a scary place to be. I didn't even realize I was going down into that deep down place the day I was out driving and almost caused a crash. I can't honestly say I didn't intentionally pull out in front of that other car, but the thought did cross my mind that it wouldn't really matter much if I got hit and died.

The most common signs of depression are sleeping less, eating less, losing weight and feelings of worthlessness. However, women are also more susceptible than men to both seasonal affective disorder – depression in the winter months due to less hours of sunlight, and atypical depression. With atypical depression, women will sleep more, eat more and gain weight. Because their depression signs aren't the norm, these women too often go undiagnosed and therefore think what they are feeling and going through is wrong and all their fault.

Depression is not normal. It's not your fault and it's not as simple as 'just getting over it.' For many women developing a new awareness and a self-care routine is a first step to finding their way back to remembering who they are really meant to be.

But for others, it's more serious. It wasn't until the night I found myself sitting on my closet floor crying because I couldn't find the key to the gun cabinet, thinking I really am a failure if I can't even pry this locked cabinet open with a screwdriver, that I realized how bad off I was. I was trying to convince myself I wasn't crazy because I wasn't even after the guns. I wanted the locked pain pills that were inside. I wanted sleep. I needed sleep. I had been up for days and thought if I just took one pain pill I could rest. If I took two maybe I'd actually sleep. But if I waited till the kids left for school I could take three, maybe four.

Call it divine intervention or simply a moment of clarity, but I came to the point where I felt as if I were outside my body looking at myself in the closet. I was actually sitting there plotting my own suicide and how to avoid having the kids be the ones to find me! I realized just how badly I needed help. Get up, I told myself. Go outside. For that night and many nights later I slept outside on my front porch until a friend rescued me and got me the help I needed.

Based on the National Institute of Mental Health website, signs of serious clinical depression include:

*Thoughts of harming yourself or your children

*Considering leaving your children and running away because they'd be better off without you

*Episodes when it is physically impossible to get out of bed and function through normal daily activities

*Feelings of hopelessness

*Sadness that is so deep and heavy you feel unable to move

If you have any of these signs, then please ask for help. You are not alone. You are not bad. You are not wrong. Asking for help is the most precious gift you can give yourself and your family. If you are afraid or don't know how to ask, highlight this passage in this book and hand it to someone you trust. If you don't know whom to trust anymore, give this to your doctor. You are worth it! You are not the negative samskaras that have taken a hold of you.

Depression is a temporary physiological state. It is not who you are.

You are a woman of grace and beauty. Inside you is a spark of the divine that shall once again shine and radiant in all directions.

Believe me, she's in there. It's time to let her out.

Meditation vs. Medication

Good yogis don't get depressed. Good yogis don't need medication. Medication is for the weak.

I believed those lies and it almost destroyed me.

During the immediate aftermath of my husband walking out on our family, I fell apart. I couldn't function in simple day-to-day tasks. Eating was impossible. Sleep didn't happen. I couldn't stop crying. It all came to a head one afternoon in the backyard with Kid 1 and his teenage buddy as witnesses.

For some reason I decided I had to mow the backyard and it had to be done at that exact moment despite my lack of sleep, energy and mental capacity. Except the mower wouldn't work.

Kid 1 tried to help me get it started, but I was so far gone from rational thinking all I could do was huddle under a tree to cry and scream. Without me realizing it, my son's friend went inside the house and called his mom.

"Ms. Jen needs help."

As Christy walked around to the back of my house I saw her and began lashing out at her, too. She stood there calmly and listened to me, and then she hugged me. I fell against her and sobbed on her shoulder for I don't know how long.

She led me over to a chair and we sat and talked. When she first suggested I might need to see a doctor I once again got angry. Eventually I exhausted my screaming and my tears and she sat with me while I called the doctor and scheduled an immediate appointment.

I found a counselor who diagnosed me with PTSD, Post Traumatic Stress Disorder. Again, I lashed out at her and told her that was a bit extreme. I'm not a soldier on a battlefield.

She helped me see, though, that trauma is trauma and my body's physiology was reacting to a trauma. My body didn't know the difference between a battlefield attack and an attack on my marriage, my family and my life.

I accepted and began taking antidepressants that my doctor prescribed. The medication helped me begin to function in a way that allowed me to face my situation in a slightly more rational and slightly more calm way.

The antidepressants were a short-term solution to allow me to make long-term decisions.

Entire libraries are full of writings on depression, it's causes and treatments. I'm not qualified to diagnose or discuss whether medication is the right solution for you. I can only speak from my own experience.

I do want you to understand though, that if you or your doctor feel you need help, take it. Don't let pride, ego or ignorance stand in the way of becoming the woman you are destined to be. Too much is at stake for you to stifle yourself.

I Love You

The first step to discovering the real you is learning to love yourself. Not to love yourself for your flaws or despite your flaws. Truly love yourself for you, for no other reason than you are a living, breathing being.

I'd been working with a life coach for a few months to try and figure out which direction my next step in life should be. Although I originally planned to discuss career goals, my coach was intuitive enough to know I needed some fine tuning on my inner-self first.

She gave me the assignment to stand in front of a mirror every morning and say out loud to myself, 'I Love You'. Oh, come on! How corny is that? But, nevertheless, I agreed to do the assignment.

Day One I made sure no one in the house was within listening distance, I closed and locked the door, and after a few minutes of hemming and hawing I stared at the floor and mumbled a barely audible 'I Love You'.

By Day 4 I'd gotten the courage to at least look up from the floor, but I still wasn't brave enough to look in the mirror. In a grudging and sarcastic voice I said, 'I Love You'.

Damn, why was this so hard?

Finally it's Day 7 and I knew my coach would ask if I've completed the assignment at our next meeting. Once again I made sure I was alone and locked the door. This time I forced my eyes to meet the ones looking back at me in the mirror. In a strong voice I said, 'I Love You'.

'No, you don't' immediately came bouncing back to me. I

began to cry.

It's true. I didn't love myself.

On the surface, things seemed good. I was building a career, my family was healthy and happy, my relationship with my husband was still difficult but I figured as good as it was going to get. I was so full of love for everyone around me that there was no love left for me.

The negative samskaras had grabbed me in their hold and convinced me I was a fake –a phony who was just keeping busy enough so no one would realize I wasn't anything special.

I had believed my own lies.

If your best friend told you that you were fat and ugly, would you continue to want to spend time with her? Would you allow your child to say mean or hurtful things to another child on the playground? Of course not.

Then why do you allow yourself to speak to your spirit in that way?

We teach people how to treat us. Every time you allow a lover, coworker or friend to put you down you give them permission to do it again. You say it's okay. I'm not worth your respect or your love. Go ahead, treat me badly.

It is not okay to for anyone to treat you badly! It is not okay for you to treat yourself badly!

When I had my doubts about starting my writing career again after a long break of raising babies, my mom reminded me there are enough other people in the world to put me down and watch me fail. I don't need to be one of them.

So how do we counteract falsehood and stay strong against those waiting for us to fail? By speaking the truth and staying strong within ourselves.

Change Your Thoughts

Psychology Today Magazine estimates the average person has between 25,000 and 50,000 thoughts per day. Most we don't even remember. First, become aware of how often you speak non-loving thoughts to yourself. Every time you say I can't, no one cares, I don't care, I'm not, it's not worth it, no one cares anyway, I'm fat, I'm old, etc., you are saying the same thing as, 'I don't love you'.

Keep count during the day. How many negative thoughts about yourself enter your mind? Whether your number is one or 100, it's too many.

Now that you are aware, counteract each of those lies with the truth. Be sure to frame the truth in a way that focuses on the positive.

For example, 'I'm too old' becomes 'I have years of experience'. 'There's never enough money' becomes 'All my needs are met'.

Positive affirmations change your thinking patterns, therefore changing your actions and resulting in a changed life.

Energy begets energy. Instead of focusing your energy on negative samskaras, refocus and shift to a more positive outlook.

A positive affirmation practice takes, well, practice. If you have been bogged down in negativity for a long time, those samskaras are deep and it will take time to refill them with positivity. Positive affirmations work if you are willing to work them.

Forget about looking like a crazy woman posting notes to yourself or talking to yourself in the mirror. Is it really any crazier than you already feel?

To aid in changing your thought patterns, make a list of positive sayings you can repeat to yourself. Keep the list handy for working through a struggle. In the past I've written out an affirmation I'm working on and taped it to my bedroom mirror, car console, and even placed it inside my wallet where I'll see it regularly.

The more positive you think, the more positive you will become and the less likely you will be to look at your past in a negative way. Once you let go of the negativity of your past, once you are positive in your present life, the more joyful and hopeful you will be for your future.

Will money suddenly grow on trees and will your children stop whining? No, of course not. But you will begin to see the abundance of what you already have and be able to take a breath and realize that the whining is only temporary.

Numerous scientific studies have been done on the power of positive attitude. In *Growing The Positive Mind*, Dr. William K Larkin says science has proven that a positive state of mind affects your body at a cellular level. Your thoughts are actually affecting your physiology! A positive attitude is more than just pretending to be in a good mood. It is truly deep down believing in the goodness and value of yourself and your life. A positive attitude can improve your health, your relationships, your self-confidence and even affect those around you.

Positive affirmations are how we take responsibility.

So Hum

I was teaching an all-levels yoga class one day when one of my students got frustrated and said to the person on the mat next to her, "I'm too fat to do this pose."

The whole class heard her and stood there uncomfortably, unsure how to react.

"Why would you say that," I asked.

"Because I am fat" she said matter of fact.

What she was saying was partly true. She was overweight and had been working hard to lose weight for almost a year.

I stood next to her mat, took her hand, looked her in the eye and asked, "But how does saying that serve you?"

Tears filled her eyes as she realized putting herself down wasn't going to help her achieve a yoga pose, lose weight or find any of the happiness she was so desperately searching for in her life.

There are too many other people in this world willing to cut you down. Don't join them.

I ended yoga class that day with a So Hum meditation. So Hum is Sanskrit for I Am That. (So = I Am, Hum = That). It's a gentle, contemplative meditation that anyone can do anywhere, anytime.

If possible, find a quiet place to sit comfortably. Close your eyes and just notice the quality of your breath. Are you breathing fast and shallow, or full and deep? No judgment here, just awareness.

When you are ready, on an inhale silently say to yourself 'So'. On the exhale silently say to yourself 'Hum'. This might be uncomfortable or awkward at first. Stay with it. Inhale So, exhale Hum.

Eventually a rhythmic pattern will develop on its own. Allow it to flow naturally. As you breathe deeper your body and mind will become calmer. You will begin to relax. Don't panic, it's okay. Don't stop now. Give yourself permission to relax. Relaxation has probably become a foreign state to you. Notice how it feels. Give your body time here to remember this feeling and learn the desire to return to it.

Tension is who we think we should be. Relaxation is who we are.

Resist the urge to add a label such as I am a mother, I am a wife, I am a dental hygienist. 'So Hum' is all you need. *I Am That*. The mantra is complete and whole.

You are all you need. You are complete and whole.

If sitting quietly somewhere sounds impossible, make it a priority to find time in your day for just a few moments of peace.

Perhaps while you feed your baby, you can close your eyes and repeat 'So Hum'. What a wonderful gift to your child to be nourished by a calm, relaxed mother!

Close the bathroom door or your office door. Length of time is much less important than intention. For just these next few moments commit to simply breathing and being.

My secret is to pull my car over to a local park or even a safe parking lot, turn off the radio and set my cell phone timer for just three minutes. I give myself permission to take that little bit of time to breathe, relax and find myself again before returning to the responsibilities of my job and family.

I take the time to breathe because I need it. I find the time for quiet because I'm worth it. I make the time to connect with my Inner Self because I love myself. I give time to myself to remind me I AM That.

You can empower yourself with just the knowledge that the only thing you really know for sure is: I am. Any word that comes after I am is just a label and can disappear tomorrow. Strip away everything you do, everything you are responsible for, and all that is left is you.

You are.

You exist

"Something inside you emerges....an innate, in-dwelling peace, stillness, aliveness. It is the unconditioned, who you are in your essence. It is what you had been looking for in the love object. It is yourself."

- Eckhart Tolle

VIKRAM

Who are you? Make a list of the labels you have given yourself (wife, mother, fat, lazy). Now rip it up and throw the list away. Who are you now?

Do you feel you have lost yourself? If so, can you remember a time when you felt like a strong and confident woman? What was happening at that time?

When did you begin to lose yourself?

What negative samskaras have you developed? Make a list. Now tear up the list and throw it away.

Make a list of positive affirmations to replace the negative samskaras. Examples include:

I'm fat – I choose to make the healthiest choices for my body

I'm not smart enough – I believe in myself and so do others

My life is chaos – I am at peace

No one cares about me – I deserve love and I accept the love that is offered

I feel sick all the time – My body is perfectly designed to heal itself

Nothing is good enough – I am grateful for all I have

I hate ________ - I'm willing to release the anger

MEDITATION MOMENT

I Am

Practice the So Hum breathing as often as possible throughout your day, every day. Notice how you feel after breathing and repeating 'So Hum'. Allow yourself to return to that calm, peaceful feeling regularly.

Find a quiet, comfortable place to sit or lie. Place one hand on your belly and one hand on your heart. Close your eyes. First notice the pattern of your breath. Is it deep? Shallow? Smooth? Choppy?

On your next inhale, think to your self the word 'So'. On your exhale, think to yourself the word 'Hum'. Allow the Hum to be deeper and longer each time you breathe.

Stay here as long as possible. If your mind wanders and you start to think about all the other things waiting for you, simply return to your breath once again. In through the nose, and out through the nose.

Inhale So. Exhale Hum. I am.

When you are ready, bring your hands together in front of your heart and take one final, peaceful breath. This time, say out loud 'So Hum, I Am'.

Commit to carrying this calm and peaceful feeling with you throughout the rest of your day and until you return to your meditation space again.

AFFIRMATION

I am worthy of love.

I am willing to show love and to accept love.

YOUR PERSONAL NOTES

2

FIRST DO NO HARM

My first child was born after more than 24 hours of labor. Obviously being exhausted and depleted, I lay in my hospital bed and tried to get some sleep. It wasn't very long before the nurses entered my room, screaming newborn in the bassinet, and told me they couldn't get my baby to stop crying. And you think I can? You're the expert, what do I know?

One week had passed and I was an even more exhausted new and nervous mom with a newborn who was still crying incessantly. Nothing I did soothed him. He wasn't hungry, dirty or in pain. I'm convinced I'm already a failure as a mother and my new precious bundle of joy hates me.

I'd hit a brick wall and as I fought to try and nurse my screaming baby I broke down and sobbed. I couldn't do this. It's too hard.

My mom walked into the room, took the baby from me, and said, "Go take care of yourself first."

With just those words, my mom gave me permission to take 30 minutes for myself to take a shower, eat a hot meal and breathe. It was exactly what I needed yet would have never allowed myself. That short break allowed me to clear my head and return to my baby a better, stronger mom.

When is the last time you put yourself first? Has it been that long?

As women, our nature is to nurture those around us. We are the caretakers and we assume that role without even being asked.

Women are the ones who care for aging parents. Even if a woman works full time outside the home, she will rearrange her schedule to attend school events and parent teacher conferences. If the kids are sick then it's usually the mother who gets up in the middle of the night. And when mom is sick, well, too bad. The show must go one, so we drag ourselves out of bed and continue with our responsibilities because who else will do it?

But at what point does being the caretaker of your family morph into becoming the martyr for your family?

There is no less honor in allowing yourself a sick day when you have the flu than there is in staying up all night cleaning up after a vomiting child. You are not selfish for letting the laundry sit dirty one more night while you go to bed early and catch up on some much needed sleep.

How you treat yourself is a direct reflection of how you allow others to treat you.

Look around your home and your life to the other living beings surrounding you. Look at your children, your pets, even your plants. You take the time to feed them healthy foods. You nourish them with clean, fresh water. You encourage their growth by allowing the kids and dogs outside to run and move their bodies. You place your plants in an area where they will get maximum sunlight.

You work hard every day to make sure your children, your animals and your plants are thriving. You deserve to put as much effort into making sure you are thriving as well.

It's not selfish to take care of yourself. It's necessary and vital to becoming the best woman you can be.

The self-care I'm talking about isn't trips to the spa, weekly manicures and facials. That's not possible for most overburdened, over busy women I know. Those are luxuries we treat ourselves to occasionally. Those are not the basic daily needs that we require to survive.

What I'm asking you to focus on are the five non-negotiable needs every woman needs. These are our most basic needs for survival:

1. Drink water
2. Eat something green
3. Get some rest
4. Break a sweat
5. Stand strong

Drink Water

Water is the essence of life. The Earths surface is 71% ocean water, not including fresh water lakes and rivers. The human body is approximately 60% water with the brain being composed of 70% water and the lungs being nearly 90% water.

Water helps digest food, transport waste and control body temperature. Waters ability to dissolves substances is what allows cells to utilize the valuable nutrients, minerals and chemicals in the biological processes.

Lack of water actually causes water weight gain. Not enough water also has been shown to cause premature aging, wrinkling, memory damage and decreased flexibility.

By the time you notice you are thirsty, you're already dehydrated. Reaching for caffeinated, carbonated or sugared drinks to quench your thirst only increases your body's dehydration. You need fresh, clean water.

After sleeping all night, your body tissues are dehydrated. The energy boost you get from coffee is at the same time depleting your body of water reserves, essential minerals and electrolytes.

Coffee and other caffeinated drinks provide a quick energy boost by stimulating the adrenal glands. The adrenal glands release hormones to break down stored sugar and release it into your blood stream giving you a quick shock to the system and a sense of alertness. However, you now have caused abnormal blood sugar levels in your body, which will lead to a big swing of energy followed by a huge crash that leaves you lethargic and fatigued again.

Soda is not a better alternative to coffee. In fact, sodas have been proven to cause weight gain, which, in turn, can lead to Type 2 Diabetes, leach calcium from your bones, and are the most highly acidic drink you can buy. Sodas change the pH level in your body, a known cause of disease.

Diet sodas are no better. Although diet sodas don't have the high calories of regular soda, when a diet soda enters your system the artificial sweeteners break down into methanol and then break down further into formaldehyde. Formaldehyde is what is used to fill dead bodies.

I'm not going to tell you that you have to give up your coffee or soda drinking habit. You are a smart, intelligent woman and can make your own health decisions. I am going to ask you to consider adding more water, and specifically, adding more water with fresh lemon into your day.

Fresh lemons stimulate the livers natural enzymes to assist the process of dumping toxins out of your body. By starting your day with a tall glass of water with lemon you are not only rehy drating your body, but also providing antioxidants, electrolytes and vitamin C.

If you prefer a hot drink in the morning, add the lemon to some warm water for a morning tea. Begin your day with a beverage that is fresh and clean. Continue drinking water as often as possible throughout the day. If you must have coffee or soda, try having a glass of water first. You might find your desire for the caffeinated beverage disappears once you properly rehydrate yourself.

Every morning, every day, every time you think 'I'm tired' or 'I'm hungry', first have a glass of water.

Eat Something Green

Stop looking at the number on your bathroom scale. The number on the scale is not a reflection of who you are, it does not reflect your intelligence, your compassion, your humor or your beauty. The number on the scale is not a reflection of how strong and capable you are.

Americans spend billions of dollars on diet programs and diet products. Diets don't work. If a diet worked we wouldn't need such a billion dollar industry built up around it. The diet industry is trying to convince you their program is the best way to eat. They are wrong. There is no one right way for everyone to eat. You are an individual with your own needs. Get off the diet track now.

The Centers For Disease Control say eating disorders affect an estimated 7 million American women. Eating disorders also affect another 1 million American men.

An eating disorder is so much more than physical. It includes the extreme emotions, attitudes and behaviors surrounding food and weight.

However, eating patterns and eating disorders actually fall along a spectrum. On one end you'll find what we most commonly think of when we use the term eating disorder; anorexia and bulimia. These are eating disorders with compensatory behavior (purging, laxative use, refusal to eat, etc.). The other end of the spectrum is binge eating without the self-imposed negative consequences. In the middle is healthy, balanced eating and attitudes toward food. Everyone falls somewhere along this spectrum.

My sister and I both struggle with our weight, yet in very different ways. I am an emotional eater. When there is stress, my instinct is to start shoving food in my mouth, especially comfort foods like carbs and sugar. My sister is the opposite. She almost has a fear of food and gaining weight. I've had many conversations with her explaining how a body needs a certain amount of calories each day to function properly and drastic calorie restriction is not healthy, nor will it cause long-term weight loss. She, on the other hand, will remind me that a pint of chocolate peanut butter cup ice cream has never solved a problem. Yes, it might provide some immediate comfort and relief, but like most addictions, in the long run it only causes more problems. Food can be a cure or a bandage depending on how we use it and what foods we choose.

Food is not the enemy. Our attitude toward food is a reflection of our attitude toward ourselves. If we eat a bad food, we must be bad. If we deprive ourselves of food then we must be strong. Our relationship toward what we eat has gotten so skewed that eating simply to nourish our body and feed our cells has gotten lost.

Diets don't work. When you are focused on depriving your

body of what you think it enjoys, you can't be aware of what it needs. It's easier to continually be on a diet and eat how someone else tells you to eat than it is to trust yourself and follow your body's innate intelligence for what it needs. Your body needs fresh, whole, real food. If a food comes in a box or has an ingredient label, odds are it's not real food. Eat a fruit. Eat a vegetable. Eat to nourish your body, not harm it.

Just as important as what you put in to your body is how you look at your body. Don't constantly criticize your body shape and size. Become aware of the comments you direct toward yourself: "I've got to lose weight", "My thighs are huge", "My belly is gross." Such self-criticism implies that appearance is more important than character.

Rather, focus on your relationship with food. Notice what types of food you prefer: salty, sweet, bitter (astringent). Become aware of your eating habits: when and where you eat.

My food rule is very simple: eat like crap and you will feel like crap. Believe me, it's a time tested and proven method!

Because I teach multiple classes in multiple facilities each day, I spend a lot of time in my car and, therefore, eating in my car. There's real potential to not only take the easy route and pull through a fast food drive thru, but also to not even be aware of what I'm eating because I'm focused on the driving.

There are a few habits I've developed to find a healthy eating program that works for me:

1. Prepare meals ahead of time. I pack my lunch almost daily and usually prepare my breakfast ahead of time as well. I have a calendar where monthly dinners are mapped out, making it easier to grocery shop and prepare food, but it also cuts down on those unhealthy and expensive pizza delivery calls

2. Don't deny myself anything. If I want ice cream, then

I will eat ice cream. I've found that denying myself only leads to binging.

3. Keep a food journal. A food journal is a good way to bring awareness to what you are eating and avoiding the mindless munching. Because of my controlling nature, I can get a little obsessive about writing all my foods down so I only use a food journal when I'm cleaning up my diet or trying to get back on track.

4. Own my decision to eat unhealthy foods. No one forced the ice cream down my throat. I am an adult and I made that choice. It's no one else's fault if I gain a few pounds. I made those choices.

5. Eat as clean as possible. When I am teaching kids' health and fitness classes, I remind them there is no diet soda river or fruit snack tree. Eat as close to nature as possible. An apple is better than an apple-flavored fruit snack.

6. Yes, I can hide the chocolate in the back of the pantry so I can eat it after the kids go to bed. But, I can never really hide what I eat. It will always show up on my waistline or in my energy level. What you eat in private, you wear in public.

No one can nourish you by eating for you. You've got to do the work.

Get Some Rest

I was in the kitchen crying hysterically because the kids didn't like the peanut butter and jelly Danishes I had bought for them. Not only were they a gift, but I had to carry them on my lap during a red-eye flight across the country and through a longer than expected airport lay over.

My mom picked up the Danish, took a bite, looked at me and said, "When is the last time you slept?"

I remember hearing one time that a woman should never make a major decision until after she's had a nap. Good advice. You are tired. Go rest. This problem will not seem so big after you've rested.

The Harvard Women's Health Watch found that women are significantly more sleep deprived than men. Physically, sleep deprivation can lead to high blood pressure, Type 2 Diabetes, makes women more accident prone and causes weight gain.

Both too little and too much sleep (often a sign of depression) affect hunger and satiety hormones. Just three sleepless nights is enough to increase the insulin resistance in your body.

Emotionally, sleep deprivation leads to depression, anger and irritability. For women, the emotional relief often comes in the form of tears, like deep sobbing and wailing over little things like peanut butter and jelly desserts. Which, of course, make us look crazy and even begin to wonder if we are crazy.

You aren't crazy. You are tired.

The National Sleep Foundation recommends seven to eight hours of base sleep per night for most people. A basal sleep need is what your body needs to function optimally. Yet, I don't know a single woman who averages eight hours of sleep per night.

Factor in sleep debt from sleepless nights and your sleep requirements could be even more.

It's too easy to just say go to bed earlier. The kids need clean clothes for school tomorrow, a work project is due or worry over impending issues is causing insomnia.

But you need to go to bed. For a restful night of sleep, try to:

- Eliminate caffeinated or alcoholic beverages in the evening

- Keep your evening meal/snack light

- Turn off the television, computer, smart phone or other electronic distractions

- Establish a nightly routine. Perhaps a cup of warm tea, a few pages of a book or any other soothing quiet activity you enjoy

- Accept that some chores might not get done today and that is ok

- Perform some type of physical exercise during the day to sleep better at night

If temporary insomnia is keeping you up at night, try a yogic breathing practice called Sitali breath, or cooling breath.

To begin, if possible curl your tongue (curling your tongue is genetic and you either can curl or you can't. It's not a reflection on you.) If you can't curl your tongue, purse your lips as if you were drinking through a straw.

Take a long, deep inhale through your mouth, and exhale slowly and completely through your nose. Your breathing pattern should be slow, full and deep. Don't try to force either the inhale or the exhale.

Repeat for about ten rounds, or until you feel calmer, and more relaxed.

Sitali breath is a cooling breath that creates a calming, soothing effect on both the mind and body. Because of its cooling properties, it is an excellent breathing practice for women experiencing hot flashes or anyone with symptoms aggravated by heat.

Rest breaks throughout the day are just as important as a good nights sleep. I've never been much of a napper. Even when I was pregnant I had a hard time lying down in the middle of the day and resting.

A mid-day break doesn't have to mean actual sleep. Taking just five, ten or even fifteen minutes of quiet is enough to rejuvenate yourself physically and mentally. That's long enough to place the baby down for a nap, give the toddlers some crayons, or close your office door.

Sit on the floor with your right hip touching the wall. Lie down on your left side and scoot your bottom all the way up so it's now touching the wall. Swing your legs up onto the wall, with your back flat on the floor and your legs up the wall.

This is Viparita Karani pose, also known as Legs Up the Wall. It's a restorative pose and a gentle inversion because your head is below your heart. Legs up the Wall pose is used as a therapeutic pose for everything from anxiety, headaches, menstrual cramps, insomnia, backaches and when in need of rest.

Stay in Viparita Karani as long as you can or are comfortable. If your lower back bothers you, place a folded blanket or small pillow under your hips. An eye pillow is also a nice addition to help calm your body and mind.

Don't be surprised if you start to dose off. I have a yoga student who is a paralegal during the day, and she almost always starts to fall asleep when our yoga class goes into this pose. It's okay. Her body is tired. Allowing her body rest is a gift she gives herself.

Break A Sweat

As I was working on this chapter my sister sent me a text message.

"What's up with overly friendly walking track people? Is it like walking track law or something they all have to say hi?"

It's the endorphins, I told her. Exercise makes you feel better and be a happier person. Just keep moving!

My sister had never been into exercise. But years of dealing with degenerative disc disease had left her with chronic neck pain and an assortment of prescription pain pills that no longer helped.

She was desperate for relief the day she put in her headphones, pushed play on her "angry leave me alone" playlist and started walking.

One week later I received another early morning text.

"Need something to do for exercise on days I have the baby. It's too cold to take her outside. I'm all fidgety! My body wants to go walk and I can't."

Yes! Her body wanted to move! It needed the fresh oxygen, increased heart rate and even the endorphin rush.

In her book *A Course In Weight Loss*, Marianne Williamson says "Exercise isn't some punishment you're going to have to endure as a price you pay for being thin. . . it's an aspect of right relationship with your body…your body wants to move. Give your body what it really wants, and it will give you what you really want."

Remember the instant energy boost you get from a morning cup of coffee? Exercise stimulates the production of hormones that work with your adrenal glands to increase your energy in a healthy natural way. And there's no sugar crash into lethargy after a workout!

The American Council on Exercise (ACE) says moderate physical activity most days of the week will also reduce cortisol (the stress hormone that causes weight gain), increase metabolism-boosting thyroid hormones, improve sleep and increase your libido.

What kind of exercise should you do? Anything you enjoy doing!

Many of my friends are marathon runners. They run in the heat of the summer, cold and rain. Although I teach yoga as cross training for their group, I no longer join them on their runs. I don't like to run. It feels like torture to me. My knee with a torn ACL and meniscus just can't run anymore. But a bad knee doesn't make me a bad person!

Your exercise options are endless: running, walking, cycling, group exercise classes, and, of course, yoga. The key to a long-term exercise program is to do what you have fun doing.

Obviously though, I'm partial to yoga. Yoga is a low impact form of exercise accessible to anyone. No special equipment is needed, it can be done alone or in a group setting, and all body shapes and sizes can have a successful yoga practice.

Yoga also has been proven to alleviate depression, reduce anxiety, and in a University of Utah study found to help patients control their pain response.

Although a yoga studio membership isn't in everyone's budget, yoga classes are offered everywhere now. Check your local YMCA, recreation centers, church, and adult education schools. If just starting out, find a beginner level class. Just as there are many types of exercise and many types of yoga, experiment with different classes and different teachers until you find one that suits you. Also check for exercise and yoga videos at your local library or through online streaming sites.

The type of exercise you choose is ultimately less important than that you do it. Every day, find a way to break a sweat.

Newton's Law of Inertia states that a body at rest remains at rest and a body in motion remains in motion. Practically speaking, that means if your body has been used to sitting on the couch, it will be content to stay sitting on the couch! It's up to you to take charge and get your body moving.

I know you're tired. And you haven't eaten well or drunk your water. You feel sluggish and lethargic. It's just too much energy to get up off the couch or out of bed.

You are in the grips of a vicious cycle: frustrated with your life, leading to depression, leading to not taking care of yourself, making poor food choices, feeling guilty over your choices, becoming more depressed and becoming more frustrated and unhappy with your life.

It's going to take a decision on your part that you are ready to stop this cycle. And, honestly, it's going to take some work. You can do this. Are you willing to move for just five minutes? Five minutes is all I'm asking.

Pick some sort of movement and move your body for just

five minutes. If after those five minutes you don't feel even the slightest bit better, you have permission to return to the bed or the couch. However, I guarantee after just five minutes you will feel better. So continue for another five minutes. Maybe even another five?

This five-minute technique is how I keep myself moving on days when I'd much rather huddle under the covers and hide from the world.

When the weather is nice, I like to go for a walk with the kids and the dogs in the evening. But some days, I've given too much to everyone else around me and I have no energy left for myself. The kids and dogs know our nightly routine and after dinner they all start dancing around waiting for me to grab the leash and go. Okay, I'll agree to a short walk to the end of the street and back.

Inevitably, once I get moving it feels good. The oxygen and blood are flowing and the fresh air feels good. I agree to walk up to the next turn. Before I know it we've completed our regular full route. The kids, dogs and I have all gotten some exercise. I feel better, their excess energy has been worked out, and it makes the rest of our evening smoother and calmer.

Walking is more than a way to spend some time with my kids and my dogs. Walking is very therapeutic for me. My favorite walks are the nights I go later when the heat of the day is gone and the neighborhood is quiet. Even during my darker times, in the grips of depression and hopelessness, I remember waiting and hoping for an opportunity to walk after the babies were tucked in bed for the night.

Walking alone, or with just the dogs, is my tranquility and my peace. Yes, it's the best low impact exercise there is, but it's so much more. No matter my pace, I can process the events of the day, make plans, or just daydream. It's the best therapy there is and it's way cheaper than weekly sessions with a doctor sitting on a couch. No matter what else has gone on in the past twelve hours, my nightly walks help me end my day on a peaceful note.

All truly great thoughts are conceived while walking.

■ *Nietzsche*

Just move. Begin with just five minutes if you have to. Make it non-negotiable that every day you find a way to move your body.

Tips from my sister to those who don't like to exercise:

- It doesn't matter how slow you are going. You are moving faster than if you had stayed in bed.
- It's not that you can't do it it's that you don't want to do it.
- It's not only about what your body wants, it's about what your body needs.
- People who frequent walking tracks are overly friendly early in the morning.
- Good shoes and sensible underwear are a must.
- Anything is possible with a good music playlist.
- There is sweat in a gym. It's okay. You can shower later.

- Failure is only an option if you allow it to be an option.

- No one is looking at you in the gym. Everyone has their own issues to work on and they don't care if your sweatpants are too old or too big.

- Your mind will tell you that you can't keep going long before your body will give out. You can tell your mind to shut up and keep going.

- You are way stronger than you give yourself credit for.

- It doesn't matter how slow you are going. You are moving faster than if you had stayed in bed.

Stand Strong

The most common way people give up their power is by thinking they don't have any.

Alice Walker

As women we are constantly trying to meet the needs of everyone around us. Whether you are a full-time working woman or a stay-at-home working mom, we feel it's our obligation to fill a position on a PTA committee, bake treats for the soccer team or volunteer for the extra work assignment no one else wants. Our attitude is if I don't do it, then who will?

I don't know who will fill the PTA position if you don't, but I do know you aren't valuing yourself, your time and your energy if you say yes when you mean no.

How often do you say yes to a request you really don't have the time or the desire to fulfill? When you do say no, do you feel a need to apologize or make excuses?

Say what you mean and mean what you say.

When I felt like I was being bullied by my boss at work, my mom reminded me to stand up for myself. Don't give your power away and allow anyone to make you feel inferior.

In yoga I teach my students that the source of their power lies inside them physically situated around their stomach area, their third chakra. From a purely physical standpoint, when you are stronger through your core muscles your entire body is stronger. You will be able to run faster, move quicker and your back will be better supported in anything you choose to do.

From society's perspective, a firm belly is considered sexually attractive and we women are obsessed with a flat stomach. Rather than doing hundreds of crunches for tighter abs (which doesn't work anyway) to make ourselves more appealing to the opposite sex, I propose we strengthen our inner core to increase our own personal power and our power in the world we live in.

I'm not looking at how flat or puffy your belly is. I'm looking deeper. How strong are you? Are you leaning on external sources rather than holding yourself up? Can you stand firm in the face of adversity, staying true to yourself and your values?

It's no coincidence that when you say yes to something that you don't want to you feel nauseated. Those butterflies and upset feelings are your intuition telling you something is wrong. What's wrong is that you are not owning your power.

Let go of the need to please because let's face it, you're never going to please everyone anyway. So give it up.

You are a grown woman. You don't need me to give you permission to say no when you want to. You know what you want and what requests are in line with your needs, values, time and energies.

You know what you want and need. Never settle for anything less.

If you're not sure about a request that's been made of you, don't answer right away. Saying 'I need time to consider that' is a perfectly acceptable response. Don't let anyone pressure you into a different answer. If anyone tries, recognize it for what it is. They are not valuing you or respecting you. That alone should help you make your decision.

And please, can we women stop making excuses? Saying 'I'm sorry I can't because my kids are sick', 'I have to drive my mom to the doctor', 'my dog is having puppies' or any of the other hundreds of other excuses we throw out makes us sound weak and unsure of ourselves.

If the answer is no, say no. Nothing more is needed. In fact, nothing more has been asked so there's no need to give out any more information.

No, I can't fill that position.

No, I'm not accepting evening appointments at this time.

No, I won't be attending your party.

No, I'm not available to babysit.

No, I won't allow you to speak to me or treat me that way.

When you learn to stand firm to the little things; babysitting requests, work assignments or extra chores, then the bigger things will get easier to say no to.

And the important things will become easier to say yes to.

Yes, I will take time for myself today. Yes, I will apply for that promotion. Yes, I will be home early to spend time with my family.

Yes, I acknowledge my needs and wishes are important and necessary and I will make taking care of me a priority.

Ahimsa

Lisa has been a yoga student of mine off and on for three years. She would often arrive to class late and agitated. At times she'd even say it was either take a yoga class or she felt like she might kill someone. She also was struggling with weight and self-esteem issues. She had been under the care of the same doctor for years although by her own admission he wasn't helping her.

Often during class I'd see her struggling in a pose, holding her breath and forcing her body in ways it shouldn't be. She was bringing her anger and issues from her life off the mat to her time on the mat.

One Saturday morning as we sat for a short meditation I noticed her face. It was soft. She looked at peace. After class I mentioned to her that she had a different presence about her lately.

Yes, she said. I'm happier.

She had taken responsibility for herself, owned her power, and finally left her old doctor and found a new doctor who not only listened and validated her concerns but was actually offering her hope and help. She had also begun taking better care of her physical self via rest, water, food and exercise.

I knew she had really made a permanent change when she handed me a Christmas card after class one day. Inside she had written:

Jennifer, thank you for teaching me to no longer treat myself with violence.

Violence doesn't necessarily mean physical violence. Poisoning your body with unhealthy food, ignoring warning signs or symptoms of possible disease, depriving yourself of rest, or allowing others to dictate your decisions are all examples of violence to yourself.

The heart of yoga philosophy comes from the The Yoga Sutras of Patanjali. Written about 200AD, the ancient sage Patanjali laid out an eight-fold path for right living. The first step on the path is what he calls the Yamas social behaviors for how you behave and treat others. Of the Yamas, the first is Ahimsa, which means nonviolence.

Nonviolence is more than 'Don't hurt yourself or others'. The broader view is consideration, compassion, and do no harm. Do no harm to others, and do no harm to yourself.

By not properly taking care of your physical body you are harming yourself. By not properly taking care of your needs, wants, and desires you are harming your inner spirit.

You need this. Your body craves it, your mind craves it and your soul craves it. By making these five items a priority every day without exception, you will begin to feel better and you will begin to become a new person.

Once you begin to take care of yourself and show your physical body kindness your inner spirit will begin to heal and you will once again feel healthy, whole and strong.

I know you're busy. I know you don't have any extra money in your budget. And, quite frankly, you are too tired to even think about exercise.

I understand. The energy you've been putting into everyone and everything around you has depleted you. Without even realizing it you have begun to wither and weaken.

Today you don't have the energy to completely revamp your diet and leave your job that you hate. Can you be willing to consider it? Just for today?

Rather than focus on 'I should give up coffee', change your script to 'Just for today, I am willing to drink a glass of water with lemon.'

Rather than worry about how to pay for a gym membership, change your focus to 'Just for today, I am willing to go for a walk around the block.'

We remove the initial hurdle of change simply by being willing to do something. Then, breaking it down to "just for today" allows us to focus on the now and not get caught up in long-term thinking and worry.

Are you willing, just for today, to begin to heal yourself?

VIKRAM

In what ways have you been violent towards yourself?

What is stopping you from practicing ahimsa towards yourself?

Are you willing to, just for today, cut down on caffeine and chemically laden drinks and replace them with fresh water? Go today, buy and cut up the lemon slices for your water.

Are you willing to, just for today, nourish your body with healthy unprocessed foods?

Are you willing, just for today, to get a good nights sleep and take a rest break during the day? Make rest a priority.

Are you willing, just for today, to move your body in a form of physical exercise you enjoy? Today, take a walk.

Are you willing, just for today, to own your power?

How does owning your power make you feel?

Which of the five non-negotiables is the most difficult for you to accomplish daily? What changes are you willing to make to make to begin caring for yourself?

Be willing and ready to repeat these five non-negotiables to-morrow.

What do you need to put in place today to make possible completing these five non-negotiables tomorrow? Put it in place now.

MEDITATION MOMENT

See Yourself Well

Find a comfortable, quiet place to sit. If your lower back, hips or knees bother you to sit for extended periods, try prop ping yourself up on pillows, a yoga bolster or folded blanket.

Close your eyes. Bring your hands to your knees palms down to ground you. Become aware of the pattern of your breath. Don't force it, or make judgments. Just notice each inhale and each exhale.

When you feel like you've found a comfortable breathing pattern, begin to form an image in your mind of what a healthy life looks like. What do you see?

If body size or shape is the first thing you focus on, that's okay. Notice it and move on. Try to see what activities represent a healthy life to you. Perhaps you are outside playing ball with your kids. Taking a hike through the woods without getting winded. Or maybe even long-term health and you are enjoying a day at the zoo with your grandchildren.

Sit with this image as long as you are comfortable. See this image as your reality. When you are ready, take a deep breath in, and exhale through your mouth to relieve any last bit of tension. Slowly open your eyes.

Commit to carrying this peaceful feeling and healthy lifestyle with you throughout the rest of your day and until you return to your meditation space again.

AFFIRMATION

I love myself enough to make sure my daily needs are met.

I give myself permission to seek out and enjoy a healthy body, mind and spirit.

SURYA NAMASKAR

(SUN SALUTATIONS)

In a vinyasa-style yoga class, poses are linked together in a flowing pattern. When combined with mindful breathing, the vinyasa becomes a graceful movement linking together mind, body, and spirit.

Surya Namaskar, known in English as Sun Salutations, is the core of vinyasa classes because they increase your heart rate, heat up the body, practice linking movement to breath and move your spine through its full range of motion both forward and backward.

Made up of 12 poses, the beauty of the full Surya Namaskar series is that it is an excellent warm up before your regular exercise routine, or it can be performed on its own anytime, anywhere. One of my marathon-running friends does a couple rounds of Surya Namaskar before her races to get her muscles warm and ready to run.

To practice Surya Namaskar (I've given both the Sanskrit and English names of the poses where applicable):

1. Begin standing at the front of your mat with your hands together at your chest. (Tadasana/Mountain Pose)
2. Inhale as your raise your arms overhead stretching the sides of your body.
3. Exhale as you bring your hands to the mat, bending your knees as much as necessary to be sure there is no discomfort in your

lower back. (Uttanasana/ Forward Fold)

4. Step your right foot back, dropping the knee down. (Lunge)

5. Step your left foot back, dropping the knee down and inhale forward to a kneeling push-up position. (Plank)

6. Bending your elbows and hugging them tight to your body, exhale and slowly lower yourself to the ground, keeping your belly off the ground as long as possible. (Chaturanga/ Low Push Up)

7. Keeping your legs and hips on the ground, inhale as you lift your chest up and forward bending at the waist, but again being sure there is no discomfort in the low back. Keeping elbows bent is fine. (Bhujangasana/ Cobra)

8. Exhale as you push the hips back against the heels, curling your toes, then lifting your hips high to the ceiling. You will look like an upside down V here. (Downdog)

9. Drop the left knee down, and bring your right foot forward between your hands. (Lunge)

10. Bring the left foot forward, exhale and slowly straighten your knees as much as possible into a forward fold. (Uttanasana/ Forward Fold)

11. Bend your knees, inhale, and straighten your body to standing, once again lifting the arms overhead.

12. Exhale and bring the hands back together in a prayer position in front of your chest. (Tadasana/ Mountain) Pause a moment for a breath. Repeat the entire series beginning with the left leg.

As you progress and get stronger, you might try practicing Surya Namaskar stepping back onto your toes rather than dropping your knees down. Take your time, move as slowly as you need to, and make any modification necessary to make Surya Namaskar fit your body.

What's most important is that you move your body and you enjoy the movement.

1.
2.
3.
4.
5.
6.
7.
8.
9.
10.
11.
12.

YOUR PERSONAL NOTES

3

EXCAVATE YOUR SELF

Something happens to a woman when she enters her fortieth decade. It's as if she's been sleep-walking through her life: getting married, raising babies, building a career, making a home, and then she suddenly wakes up. She takes a look at the life she's built. She looks in the mirror and doesn't even recognize herself. Is that gray hair? Are those wrinkles around the eyes? What happened and why wasn't I paying attention?

She walks downstairs and surveys the chaos. She looks across to her family who are waiting rather impatiently for her to just do all the same things she's usually done. I mean, really, Mom wouldn't inconvenience us for her own needs would she?

She takes one last look in the mirror and confirms she doesn't like what she sees. She's not even sure what she sees. Turning to her family, who have turned up the volume on their demands, she gathers her voice and announces, "Oh, hell no!" Hell no! I will not be at your beck and call anymore. Hell no! I will not push my needs aside to take care of yours. Hell no! I will no longer live the life someone else wants me to live.

Watch out world. The Goddess has awoken!

Women in their forties suddenly develop an affinity for bright red nail polish. They begin digging around the back of their closet for high heels that were boxed up a long time ago.

The fear of making a major life change suddenly becomes much less scary than the fear of staying exactly where you are. It is time to take back control of your life.

"Nature gives you the face you have when you are twenty. Life shapes the face you have at thirty. But it is up to you to earn the face you have at fifty."

-- Coco Chanel

In her book *Feelings Buried Alive Never Die*, Karol K. Truman explains the Law of Control. Simply put, the degree of control we have in our life is in direct proportion to our mental health. The more in charge of our decisions and choices we feel we are, then the higher our self esteem and confidence will be.

In psychology this is called internal vs. external locus of control. Those with a high internal locus of control take responsibility for their actions and their life. Women who believe they are victims of their circumstances, who tend to blame others for their struggles, have an external locus of control.

A woman who feels her life is out of control is absolutely right. Whatever you believe becomes your reality. Even if everyone around you is telling you different, your current state of mind won't allow any information that is incompatible with your current perception of reality.

A woman with an external locus of control isn't owning her power. She has given it away. Deep down she knows she's given her power away, but she isn't aware enough yet to take it back. Right now she's too busy blaming others for her circumstances.

The blame game can be fun, for a while. It's a guaranteed way not to have to focus on yourself and your culpability. But, the blame game also gets weary. It's exhausting continually coming up with new people to blame or new reasons to keep blaming the same person.

Eventually, when you're ready to begin finding yourself

again, you've got to stop looking at others and start looking at yourself.

The first benefit when you stop blaming others is you no longer are a victim. Celebrate! You are not a victim!

Now comes the real work. Once you are no longer a victim, it's time to take responsibility. When we leave denial behind, we might have to actually admit that we in some way contributed to our own misery.

You have made mistakes in your life. So have I. Like me, I bet you've made the same mistake more than once, maybe more than twice. We all make mistakes, but the second, third, or fourth time we make the same mistake it's called a choice. It's no longer anyone else's fault. We walked into this mess with our eyes wide open, knowing full well what would happen.

And now it's time to take responsibility.

You might be in a difficult situation. But you are not in an impossible situation. What you did to get yourself here is no longer relevant. How are you going to move forward from here?

Stop Hiding

Healing only happens when we come out of hiding. The secrets you hold inside you might be shocking to those around you, but they aren't insurmountable. The secrets you hold inside you are like a cancer growing ugly black tumors. Each time you swallow the truth, you feed the blackness.

But the thing about secrets is, they only have power over you as long as you keep them a secret. Once you decide to set the secret free, your burden is released and you will be lighter and freer.

I was married to my husband for twenty-three years. My husband was not a bad man. But, at times, he was a sick man. The cycle of addiction has been passed down in his family for generations. Despite his desire not to allow it to continue, he has had his battles with alcoholism.

I spent a lot of years angry and hurt by his drinking. And even more years trying to hide the fact that my husband would rather stop off at the local bar with the guys than come home to me and the kids.

What I eventually realized is that my life is not defined by his actions. My life does, though, become shaped by my reaction to his actions. I'm sad to say some of my reactions were not honorable, and they certainly weren't helpful.

His drinking is his truth to tell. It's not about me. My story, my reaction to his drinking, is all about me. It's my story to own.

What happens to the spirit of an already over-tired and depressed woman when faced with hurt and disappointment? Would I know enough to choose to take care of myself and stay calm and rational in the midst of an emotional storm? Sadly, no. I wasn't aware at the time that I had the choice to take care of myself and own my God-given power.

Instead, during my darkest days I chose to point blame. Because I didn't love myself, because I wasn't practicing ahimsa, I chose to retaliate in hopes of causing him some of the deep pain that I was feeling. I allowed the attention of other men to build my self-esteem and cause jealousy with my husband. My self-esteem was so low that my sense of worth came from external sources rather than inside me. I had lost myself and didn't even know how to begin finding my way back again.

The only thing I accomplished was plunging myself further into depression, and pushing my husband and me farther apart. We were two hurting people, both hiding behind the lies we'd told ourselves rather than facing the truth together.

When my husband and I were in the midst of our marital crisis, I didn't feel safe telling anyone around me what was happening. I was afraid people would no longer love me if they knew my secrets. I was afraid people would judge me if they knew his secrets.

I spent a long time holding my breath, afraid to speak the truth of what was happening to us. The more I hid the worse the situation got. The more I denied the truth, the worse I felt. The longer I kept quiet, the greater the distance grew between my husband and me.

Once the burden became too much for us both to bear, the truth came rumbling out. As we cleaned up the fallout, our self-created mess hung over our heads a little less each day. The truth was out there. By telling each other what was going on, and why, we took away the power anyone else had over us.

My fear of others judging me was really my internal voice talking to me. My spirit was screaming at me to find myself, take care of myself and heal myself. Once I listened, I began to face the truth and step onto the path of self healing.

Did some people judge us and feel entitled to share their opinion although it wasn't asked for? Of course. People judge others to try to make sense of their own lives, so they can make their own issues fit nicely into whatever lies they've told themselves. It's very important to be discerning in who you share with. Share only with people who have earned the right to hear your story.

Those who have a stake in your well being won't judge you.

Years later, with the benefit of hindsight, I see now that once our secrets were exposed, the people who cared about us didn't judge us. Instead, they reached out a hand to help us.

Coming out of hiding isn't easy. Speaking the truth takes courage and the strength that only comes from deep down in that place where your Spirit lives. That place untouched by the drama and trials of your life.

The unconscious mind gives out physical signals when you are hiding a truth. People will repeatedly clear their throats before saying something that makes them uncomfortable. Notice how you very briefly hold your breath when you are about to divulge a secret or say something you are afraid to say. The breath is actually how your larynx makes sound. The mouth forms the letters, but the larynx, situated in the throat, is the source of the sound. Deb Shapiro, in *Your Body Speaks Your Mind*, says the throat is the link between the body and the head, between the heart and the mind. She goes on to say that the throat is where you express, or repress, your feelings.

Using your voice is how you put your willingness to own your power into effect. Finding and using your voice takes courage and strength. You will be infinitely more powerful when you release the fear and speak your truth. Every baby step of acknowledgement, every admission of imperfection and every concession to reality brings us a little bit closer to wholeness within ourselves.

Are you willing to be healed? See the truth, speak the truth and be the truth.

"The truth will set you free, but first it will piss you off."

-- Gloria Steinem

Sit Quietly With Yourself

We live in a very noisy world. We've become so accustomed to the constant interruption of news streams, social media sites and chatter of those around us that most of us feel uncomfortable in silence. The noise we allow into our lives creates a diversion so that we don't have to learn to be with ourselves. If I'm even partially focused on whatever is blaring in the background of my life, I'm not fully focused on my life.

I can't find out who I really am, I can't express my authentic Self, I can't change my life to live in a way that honors my Self, until I get quiet, get focused, and become aware.

"We need to find God, and he cannot be found in noise and restlessness. God is the friend of silence. See how nature - trees, flowers, grass - grows in silence; see the stars, the moon and the sun, how they move in silence.... We need silence to be able to touch souls." – Mother Teresa

Meditation is the seventh limb of yoga. Known as dhyana, meditation is often incorrectly thought to mean a way of stopping all thoughts. That's not possible. Trying to empty the mind is like asking the ocean to stop making waves. It can't happen. With meditation it is possible to make the waves smoother, quieter, and more soothing.

Patanjali taught that we all have what he calls a "drunken monkey mind." The drunken monkey swings through the trees from branch to branch in a random pattern with no connection or time to stop and rest. Our mind works the same way. The constant internal chatter you have with yourself all day flows from thought to seemingly random thought so that eventually you don't even remember what you were supposed to be focused on.

Meditation is one tool to quiet the chatter, which will allow your truth to come through.

I understand meditation may have some foreign or scary perceptions to you. I promise you don't have to go sit on a mountain top, chant, or burn incense. You just have to be willing to sit with yourself quietly.

Living where I do in the Bible-belt South, meditation also has some false religious stereotypes. My teacher explained to me that prayer is talking to God. Meditation is listening to His answer. Long-time meditators have often described their meditation practice as feeling as if they were sitting in the hands of God.

When I teach beginner's yoga classes I sometimes begin with ninety seconds of quiet meditation. Those ninety seconds can be pure torture for someone who is used to always being on the go and thinking ten steps ahead. If ninety seconds of quiet feels like the longest ninety seconds of your life, you need more periods of ninety seconds of quiet!

There is no right or wrong way to meditate. To begin, find a quiet place to sit comfortably. Let go of the pictures you have in your head of people sitting in full lotus position with their hands in prayer. Sit however feels best to you

I prefer to close my eyes, but I know others feel safer keeping their eyes open, perhaps fixed on an object in front of them. Notice your breath flowing in and out of your body. Become aware of what parts of your physical body are holding tension. Can you relax your shoulders, your neck, your back, your hips? Notice how you begin to feel when you relax. Is this a comforting state for your body? Or do you feel slightly panicked like you should be moving and doing? Don't judge any feelings or emotions that arise. Just become aware.

That was about ninety seconds. How did you do?

I always give new meditators the same advice; don't make it hard! Don't put any pressure on yourself to sit for a certain amount of time or achieve a certain state of relaxation. Meditation is your time to be quiet. Your time with no expectations of you. Your time to simply be. Ten minutes is great or ten breaths is great. Your mind, body and spirit will appreciate it.

If sitting quietly just isn't possible for you, change what your meditation time looks like. Perhaps go for a quiet walk in the afternoon to clear your head, or take a short break between appointments to focus on your breath. Even dusting the living room can be a meditative practice if you focus your complete awareness to the feel of the cloth in your hand, the motion of your arm as you wipe, and the smell of the polish you use.

Meditation is nothing more than paying attention on purpose even when performing the most mundane aspects of your life.

Once you become more comfortable with a meditation practice, your body and your mind will begin to crave it. With a large family and a small house, sitting quietly on my meditation cushion isn't always possible. Instead, I've developed my own private car meditation practice.

I'll leave for work just a few minutes early and stop off at a local park or safe parking lot. I set the timer on my cell phone for five or ten minutes, turn off the radio, and begin to breathe deeply. It's enough to quiet my mind and help me set a calm, peaceful tone to my day. When I'm feeling like my life is really hectic I'll pull my car over before going home to multiple kids all needing chauffeured to multiple destinations. Just a few minutes to realign and quiet myself allows me to go home a happier, more relaxed mom.

Not only do I benefit from my meditation, but my family and those around me benefit as well. If you think meditation won't work for you, give it a try for sake of those around you.

Get The Crazy Out

"You don't have to act crazy anymore –
we all know you were good at that."

I Heard God Laughing: Poems of Hope and Joy

Daniel James Ladinsky

Everyone needs a way to get the crazy out. Finding a creative outlet is essential to a well-rounded and more joyful life. Studies have shown lack of creativity leads to depression, apathy, and increased stress.

In a perfect world my creative spirit would shine as I sing back up for Tina Turner on her world tour. Unfortunately, my creative skills don't include the ability to sing. And I don't enjoy crafts that require glue guns, pink tulle or tying bows. I'm not a crafty person. But I do have a need to be a creative person.

To create simply means to bring into existence. Even if you aren't a crafty person, your Spirit still has a desire to create things.

Creative pursuits include more than just art. Photography, woodworking, jewelry making, home decorating, fashion, even developing business plans are creative endeavors.

My mom's creativity shined in the kitchen. She never made

just a grilled cheese sandwich. Her cooking always had that little something extra that made it special and memorable.

Knowing how much my mom loved to cook and experiment with new ingredients, my cousins brought her a jar of specialty truffles on one of their last visits to her as she was dying of cancer. What my cousins didn't know was I am not creative in the kitchen and had no idea what to do with these truffles that I'm sure cost more than a couple weeks of my salary. Even though she was entering hospice the next day and could barely swallow, my mom really wanted a meal prepared with the truffles.

As I stood in her kitchen looking at all the utensils she loved to collect and use, I was so nervous I was practically shaking. I have no idea what to do with a truffle, what if I ruin it? This will be the last meal she eats in her own home, what if she doesn't like it? This is crazy. I'm not the cook of the family. I don't know what to do.

Convinced I was failing in fulfilling my moms last wish, I fought to hold back tears as I made my way upstairs to her bedroom. She looked so small lying there in her hospital bed, eyes closed, dozing under the influence of the pain meds.

As she opened her eyes and saw me standing there, she asked what was wrong. I don't know what to cook for you, I told her.

She reached for my hand, looked at me, and said "Whatever you make, just make it with love."

The pasta, garlic and truffle dinner I made that night was filled with all the love I had. And the few small bites Mom was able to swallow brought her joy in her last days. My creation, although lacking in expertise, was made with love and it made someone else happy. It made me happy.

That is why we create; to share the joy that our efforts bring to us.

When you engage in creative activities, you are channeling the energy coursing through you. When you truly love what you are doing, you'll find yourself working effortlessly, perhaps even losing track of time. When you are completely focused on what you are creating, it will feel as if you are no longer in control but rather your Spirit is working through you.

Writing is my way of getting the crazy out of my head. From the earliest time I can remember I've kept journals, first in random notebooks and later in whatever my new favorite technological gadget at the time is. Even if my voice can't sing, my heart sings as my fingers fly over the keyboard and I create a new story.

Write Your Story

You don't need to be an eloquent writer to record your own story. You just need to start writing. Writing is a left-brain activity. The left hemisphere of your brain is the rational and analytical part of your brain. When the left brain is occupied, the right brain is more free to create, feel and be intuitive.

Writing in a private journal can help you clarify your thoughts and feelings, allowing you to dig deeper inside yourself. In a journal you are free to say things you don't feel safe saying in real life. It's an objective place to process the circumstances of life, heal from your past, and move forward with intention and purpose. You can find the answers to the questions you are struggling with. I consider a private journal to be a form of meditation: a place to be quiet and allow the mind to declutter itself.

Other benefits of journaling include:

- Reduced stress
- Solve problems more effectively
- Bring closure to conflict rather than dwell on it
- Soothe troubled memories
- Self discovery
- Provide mental stimulation
- Explore your spirituality
- Connect inner thinking to the outer events of your life

Like meditation, there is no wrong way to journal. Don't put any pressure on yourself for a set amount of time or number of pages to write. Spelling, grammar and syntax don't matter in your journal. Allowing your words to be for your eyes only gives you permission to write unfiltered what you are really thinking and feeling.

Never judge what you put on the paper. Even if what you write sounds irrational and crazy, get it out. That swirling ball of frenetic energy inside you needs a safe outlet.

Suggestions for beginning a journaling practice:

- Stream of consciousness writing: Simply begin writing whatever comes to mind. Don't force the writing to be connected or even make sense, the goal is to simply get the chatter from your head onto the paper. Stream of consciousness writing is usually done for short set periods of time, perhaps ten to fifteen minutes.

- Inspirational writing: Keep a notebook full of quotes, poetry, bumper stickers or any other uplifting and motivational words you read. On difficult days you can refer back to these pages for encouragement.

- Prayers: Consider writing down your prayers as a way to offer them up to God. Once they are written, you place the power in His hands.

- Affirmations: In Chapter One I encouraged you to begin using positive affirmations to replace the negative samskaras you have developed. Some days, it's going to be really tough to fight the samskaras. Having a list of positive affirmations to refer back to will help on those days when it feels easier to just give in to the darkness.

- Chronicle: Keeping a written account of your path to a more joyful life allows you look back and see how far you've progressed

VIKRAM

What changes would you like to make in your life?

What fears do you have about making this change? What fears do you have if you don't make this change?

What secrets are you hiding? Are you willing to first be honest with yourself about your truth?

Write down your secrets. Now, burn the paper and release them.

Are you willing to safely expose your truth in order to set yourself free?

What judgments are you holding on to about yourself? Your situation?

Write down your secrets. Now burn the paper and release it.

Would you be as harsh with a friend sharing her secrets with you?

When do you feel the most creative?

What activity brings you joy?

Are you willing to commit time in your life to carving out more creative time? Schedule creative time today.

Find a notebook to use as your personal journal. Or use a journal app on your favorite electronic device. Write in it daily.

MEDITATION MOMENT

Living Your Values

Find a comfortable position in a quiet place. Close your eyes and simply breathe. Soften your face and relax your jaw. Allow the tension in your shoulders to slide away. Your back is straight yet relaxed. Your hips, knees and legs feel light and open.

Your physical body is relaxing and opening, almost sinking into the space around it. When you are ready, turn your attention inward. What do you feel? What emotions arise as you sit quietly?

Allow a word that represents one of your core values to surface. Perhaps truth, loyalty, or honor. There is no wrong answer. There's no need to force anything here. Patiently wait for your word to bubble to the surface.

Once you find your word, focus on it. See the letters in your mind. Silently repeat the word to yourself. Notice if your focus on this word causes any physical changes in your body – perhaps a tightening of certain muscles or a change in your breathing pattern. If so, focus on your breath once again to encourage your body to relax.

Visualize what this word means to you. How or where does it appear in your life? Or is it lacking in your current situation? How would you like to manifest more of this word in your life? Visualize yourself living this word.

This word represents your core values, a part of your

authentic self. When you are ready, bring your hands together in front of your heart. Take a big breath in through the nose, and on the exhale say this word out loud.

Commit to carrying this word and this peaceful feeling with you throughout the rest of your day and until you return to your meditation space again.

AFFIRMATION

I speak the truth so that I may hear the truth. I face my fears so that I may release my fear. I invite change so that I may experience a positive change in my life.

JOURNAL WRITING PROMPTS

Here are a few ideas to inspire your writing time. Don't let these suggestions limit you. Let your imagination and your writing run wild and free!

1. Who is the most influential person in your life right now?

2. Write a letter to your best friend from high school describing your current life.

3. What made you laugh today?

4. Describe ten things that make you happy.

5. Write a letter to yourself from the point of view of your spouse or significant other.

6. Who or what upset you today? Write what you would like to say to that person.

7. Write down five short-term goals and five long-term goals.

8. Take a look at your surroundings. Where do you see beauty? Describe it. Where can you create more beauty?

9. Notice a stranger next time you are out in public. Make up their life story.

10. In what ways are you similar to your mother? In what ways are you different?

11. Write a letter of apology to someone you feel you should apologize to.

12. If you could live anywhere, where would it be? Why? How would your life be different?

13. What is the last thing you did solely for yourself? What would you like to do for yourself in the future?

14. If you could pick one talent or skill what would it be? What would you do with your talent?

15. Write a letter to God. Begin Dear God and write everything that comes to mind.

YOUR PERSONAL NOTES

4

HONEY, WE'RE ALL GUILTY OF SOMETHING

I don't even remember the current scandal that was being covered ad nauseam in all the media. I do remember arguing passionately with my mom about the woman's role in it. Yes, but look what *she* did! I said.

"Honey, we're all guilty of something," my mom pointed out to me.

At the time I think I was too young and naïve to really understand what she meant. Eventually I learned life isn't so black and white. There are definite shades of each that exist in all of us.

In the Sanskrit language there is no word for guilt. How amazing is that?

Those of us born into the Judeo-Christian religion know all about guilt. We were lucky enough to be born with original sin. Guilt allows our actions to manifest as our self, who we are, rather than I did a bad thing, I am a bad person. Who we are gets confused with what emotion we are feeling. You are not your emotions! Remember who you are, who your Self is.

You may have acted in a way that was inappropriate and you feel remorse. Guilt and remorse are two very different things. The guilt occurs when you project your mistake onto yourself and either don't know what to do about it or refuse to correct it.

If left unchecked, guilt will run rampant, creating new nega tive samskaras in our mind that are so deep and so wide we will have to spend years crawling our way out of them. Guilt clouds your thinking so that you no longer even see the situation clearly. It can lead to self-hate and certainly a lack of self-confidence.

'I'm a bad person. I'm not worthy of being loved, so why bother taking care of myself?' No matter what the situation that has brought you to this point, this is exactly the time you need to be taking care of yourself. You will never release the guilt until your body, mind, and spirit are aligned with each other in the strongest, healthiest way.

Guilt extends worry about what we've done. All stress, worry, and anxiety come from living too much in the future and not enough in the present. All unforgiveness comes from living too much in the past and not enough in the present.

Even in times of strife it's possible to stay focused, stay calm, and stay present. In fact, it's the only thing we must do.

Momma Guilt

If you have children then I don't need to explain what momma guilt is. It begins the exact moment the little stick turns pink. You are now responsible for another human life. How will you ever live up to that task?

Let me just take a little pressure off you right now; at times you will fail as a mother. Accept it now, fix it when you can, and move on.

"If we are peaceful, if we are happy,

We can blossom like a flower,

And everyone in our family,

Our entire society,

Will benefit from our peace."

Thict Nhat Hanh

Even we yoga teachers struggle. I remember a typical rough day that, looking back now, I realize was so not worth it. The day started at 7 a.m. with a misunderstanding between my husband and me. In the grand scheme of life it was a minor incident and it should have ended at 7:05 a.m. But I didn't want to let it end. I was annoyed at how inconsiderate I thought he was and I wanted to be sure he knew it. So when we next saw each other for a preplanned lunch date at 1pm I was cold and distant. He didn't take the bait, which just escalated my annoyance.

By 6 p.m. I was lashing out at everyone around me. Frustrated by my own overly-scheduled day, I was feeling a lot of stress and honestly just not in the mood to be willing to do anything to relieve it. A family revolt over eating leftovers for dinner was enough to push me over the edge and make me one angry momma.

Most of my family had scattered to other parts of the house, far away from me and my impending explosion. The only one brave enough to still seek out my presence was kid number six, who was then about five years old. She insisted on helping with the dishes. I should have been grateful for the help, right? Instead I focused on how her help slowed me down and added one more burden to my day. As she wiped the table she sang her new favorite pop song. I wasn't focused on her singing. I just reminded her to pay attention to what she was doing. Sure enough as little kids do, she dropped and broke a bowl. My frustration finally boiled over and I way too harshly reprimanded her for her carelessness. She left the room in tears and I finished the dishes with the knowledge that I was the worst mom in the world.

Later, as I walked back to check on the kids' bedtime progress I again heard her singing, this time in the shower. She was belting out that same tune with complete abandon. She was happy. Despite the chaos and negativity in my home, admittedly caused by me, she stood strong and stayed true to her Spirit. Nothing and nobody were going to stop her from singing.

I stood and listened for a minute before opening the door. Again, I thought, 'What a horrible mother I am. Here I've been stomping around all day complaining and acting like a crazy lady. Someone as ungrateful as me doesn't deserve a sweet little girl who sings in the shower.'

As soon as I entered the bathroom she stopped singing and looked at me, unsure what my reaction would be. I'm sure she expected me to tell her to quit goofing around and get done.

It was my turn to make a choice. I could stay seeped in my own misery and momma guilt and dig some new samskaras. Or I could choose repentance and joy.

I reached over, grabbed a hairbrush and began singing the next verse as loud as I could. My little girl laughed, we both smiled and together we finished her bedtime routine. I apologized for being in a bad mood and she gave me a big hug.

Will my not-always-perfect mommy skills force her into therapy when she's 30? I hope not. But if it does I hope she'll remember the lesson that even though I wasn't the best mom that day, I was still a loving forgiving mom.

Children almost always love and forgive their parents. It's we moms who have a hard time loving and forgiving ourselves. Kid number Five is now almost twelve years old, yet I still get a lump in my throat when I think about what happened when he was only three months old.

It was a typical weekday evening. I was in the kitchen cleaning up from dinner. My oldest child was at the dining room table doing homework, and the other kids were outside playing. My husband was at a friend's house, having just a beer that had already lasted way longer than one drink should take.

I was only a few months postpartum, overtired and overwhelmed with taking care of five children under the age of eight and deeply angry and resentful toward my husband who was too busy feeding his addiction to help me with my needs.

Even though I knew all the safety rules, I placed the baby's carrier on top of the kitchen counter. Even though he was a wiggly baby and had a history of squirming his way down the seat I didn't buckle him in. I have no excuse. No matter how tired I was I knew better.

As I finished up the kitchen I walked outside to call the rest of the kids back in to the house. I couldn't have been on the porch more than a couple minutes when I knew something was wrong. A feeling so powerful came over me I've never been able to accurately describe it. Yet I knew I needed to get back in the house.

There, on the kitchen floor, lay my baby, facedown and not crying with a small trickle of blood coming from his nose.

There is no word for the kind of fear I felt at that moment. I scooped him up from the floor, yelled at Kid number One, remember who is only eight years old himself, to go get his dad and the rest of the kids.

I barely had time to explain as I buckled my now screaming

baby (thank God at this point he's at least crying!) into the car and sped off to the hospital.

Want to know what momma guilt is? It's when you are standing alone in the emergency room watching as your baby is strapped down and placed into a Cat Scan machine. It's being pushed aside as the doctors and nurses to try and figure out if the blood is from his nose when he fell or if he has a head trauma. Not only can I not move in to touch or comfort my scared and in-pain child, but I am the reason he is there.

I was negligent. It's my fault. I am a bad mom. Here is the proof. As I watch the doctors work I am clutching my stomach, trying to keep my composure. Every time I hear someone walking down the hallway I know it has to be the police on their way to arrest me or take my child away.

I'm not hysterical. I'm numb. I did this. I hurt my baby. Finally my mom shows up to the hospital. She pulls me aside, looks me in the eye and says "This was an accident."

Just four little words and I crumbled. I cried and said how sorry I was and please forgive me and I'm not even sure what else. Miraculously the only damage was a broken femur in two places. He'd need a cast for a couple months, but there was no head or brain injury. As bad as it was it could have been much worse.

As we waited for the pediatric orthopedist to arrive, the nurses finally handed me my baby. As I held him ever so gently so as not to hurt him further, he snuggled against me and began to nurse. My baby still loved me.

Everyone Struggles

Momma guilt is something we all can relate to and most of us are willing to share with friends. But there's that other kind of guilt too.

Maybe you know the kind I mean. The guilt that you wouldn't dare tell your friends because if they knew the truth, well, it's just too much and they'd never accept you. Guilt that makes you want to crawl under the covers and hide from God.

The kind of guilt that eats away at you, creating a darkness inside that you try to keep secret. Whether fighting an addiction, a secret affair, an abusive relationship or any of the other hundred things that could cause you to forget to first and foremost love yourself.

Guilt also is a way to berate yourself before anyone else has the chance to do so. There's no need for anyone else to punish you because you are doing a mighty fine job of that yourself.

When you engage in guilty thoughts, you are once again living in the past. If your actions have caused harm to others it's almost selfish of you to keep yourself and your thoughts focused on what happened then. You are no longer living in the moment and focused on who you are in the present. You are the only one suffering from your negative and guilty thinking.

Meditation helps release the burdens of your mind before the samskaras get too deep. Meditation also is like a reset button bringing our body and mind back to its natural state of peace and calm. When we are more at peace, we are less likely to create imaginary monsters waiting to tear us apart for our transgressions. When we are at peace, we can better avoid depression. Depression and pessimism will never solve a problem.

You can't change your shortcomings until you accept yourself despite them. Feeling guilty for your flaws is just another way you choose to treat yourself violently rather than practice ahimsa.

Once your mind is quieted you can begin the process of renewal. Catholics have confession and Baptists have a water baptism after which they are considered to be born again. St. Augustine and St. Paul were both sinners before they were saints. Even the Buddha was a flawed man before he sat under the Bodhi tree and became enlightened.

Whether your guilt is typical run-of-the-mill momma guilt, or something deeper and potentially more harmful, the physiological response to the emotion is the same.

Guilt is guilt. And it serves no one.

It's a process and it takes time. Go ahead and give yourself time to wallow. Take the hour, the day, the week if the situation deems that long. Cry, wail, prostrate yourself in the middle of the room if it helps. Then, it is over. Crawl out from under the covers and get back to your life.

Love yourself, flaws and all, right where you are. You are not perfect, but you are perfectly created.

Anger

"Anger is a poison you take hoping the other person will die."

When we get angry, especially at someone we love or trust, our brain gets all kinds of signals from the primitive flight or fight response in our body. Those signals are stored in our mem ory, and each time we dredge up those memories the same angry hormones, poisons, are sent through our body again. That's why we can still get angry about something that happened years ago.

Even if it's a daily annoyance type of anger, such as a frustrating call to customer service or disobedient children, the body sensors are alerted in the same way. The body's flight or fight response can't distinguish between a lover who has betrayed us or a boss who asks too much and gives too little.

As I was writing earlier about my guilt over my baby falling off the counter, I realized I was still holding on to some anger for my husband not being there when it happened. It's been almost ten years and I've spent so much time in self-reflection and meditation, yet dredging up that memory brought up some surprisingly still unresolved emotions. I felt my heart quicken and my breath become fast and shallow. The poisons had once again started coursing through my body.

I admit I can hold a grudge better than anyone. Want to know what was said in an argument from fifteen years ago? I can quote it verbatim. This skill has served me in no way other than creating darkness inside me. My chiropractor calls it an emotional cancer.

Allowing an emotional cancer to grow inside yourself is not practicing ahimsa. As I contemplated my unexpected reaction and latent anger over the fall off the counter incident, I realize that at the time I was so full of guilt and blame I didn't have the energy to process any anger I was also feeling. All these years later my body is still having a physical response to that incident.

Anger and guilt go hand in hand. It's rarely considered an appropriate time to express anger in the moment, so we swallow it down and repress it. Later, after time has passed and we gain a little perspective either one of two things happen. We realize the situation didn't warrant that level of anger in the first place so we feel guilty for letting feelings get so out of control. Or, the situation was worthy of our anger, yet we didn't own our power at the time so now we feel guilty for not standing up for ourselves. So now I'm angry at you and I'm angry at me.

Who am I hurting by holding on to the anger? Only me.

Forgive Yourself

You can't forgive anyone else until you first forgive yourself. Whether real or perceived, you do have things you need to forgive yourself for. Once you begin the process of forgiving yourself, you can expand that act out to those who have harmed you, again either in a real or perceived way.

I know you are thinking you shouldn't forgive the people who harmed you. They don't deserve your forgiveness. Perhaps you are right. Maybe they don't deserve it. But you deserve it. Just as with anger, the only one you are hurting by refusing to forgive is yourself. Forgiveness means you are letting go of trying to change the past.

Once you forgive, you are no longer a victim. You have reclaimed your power over the situation and over your life. You are taking the Law of Control by the tail, swinging it over your head, and saying this life is mine to live and I am ready to get back to living it!

Once you are ready to let go of the past you will begin to live in the present. And enjoy your present life.

"When obstructive thoughts arise, practice the opposite thought."
Patanjali's Yoga Sutra 2:33

Since you are now a woman who makes self care a priority, it shall be your priority to love and forgive yourself first. When those negative samskaras pop up, you know now to replace them with love and kindness. When dark emotions and thoughts creep in about someone else, you now know to replace them with love and kindness. On those days when you are just mad at the whole world, you now know to stop, breathe, and move to a place of love and kindness.

Does this sound too easy and maybe even a little Pollyana-like? Are you willing to at least try it? You have nothing to lose. Just for today, be willing to fake it until you make it. I promise, soon it will get easier. Then it will become effortless. Then it will become a part of you. Living from a place of love, compassion and joy are possible.

The Buddha called the lovingkindness mediation the antidote to fear. This meditation facilitates a positive change in attitude first in the one practicing the meditation, and then rippling out to all those around. The Buddhist tradition refers to this as a metta meditation. The same concept is found in Greek Agape, Jewish Chesed, and the Christian Bible verse Matthew 5:44; "But I say unto you, Love your enemies, bless them that curse you, do good to them that hate you, and pray for them which despitefully use you, and persecute you". Replace fear (anger, resentment, etc) with love and you shall be loved and you shall be loving.

Although there are many versions of the lovingkindness meditation, I prefer the one taught by author Sharon Salzberg, an American spiritual and meditation teacher.

First, find a comfortable, quiet place to sit. Yes, your car is acceptable. So is your bathroom when necessary. Close your eyes and focus on your breath. Allow yourself to settle into your body and into the present moment.

When ready, repeat these phrases: 'May I be safe. May I be happy. May I be healthy. May I live with ease.' Gently repeat the phrases over and over again. The specific words themselves aren't as important as the intention behind them.

In her book. *Learning To Breathe: My Yearlong Quest to Bring Calm to My Life* Priscilla Warner describes practicing the lovingkindness meditation at a workshop she attended with Salzberg. Warner learned to say the phrases in sets of three a total of four times.

The first three times the words are said for yourself to yourself. The second three times the words are said for someone who has helped you or brought joy to your life. The third set is said in honor of someone you know who is in need of healing. The final round is sent out to the universe wishing everyone everywhere a life filled with happiness, safety, health, and ease.

Everyone you meet, in their own way is struggling or suffering. Learn to love and forgive yourself first. Then you will be able to see the world in a more loving and compassionate way.

May I be safe.

May I be happy.

May I be healthy.

May I live with ease.

The Wife v. The Mistress

A Lesson In Compassion*

I have to pee when I get nervous. I'm in the car driving to meet my husband's mistress and I have to pee for the fifth time in an hour. Or maybe I just need to vomit. Probably both.

Nine months ago my husband of 23 years walked out on our family and into this woman's arms. And now she wants to meet with me. I've run through every possible scenario in my head of what she could want. What ulterior motive could she possibly have? Of course, I've also played out all the vile and nasty, but very true, words I want to say to her.

"Why would you meet with her?" my friends have asked me. "Oh, hell no, I'd tell that bitch exactly where she can go," say others.

She has no idea the nights I held crying kids who just wanted their daddy. She has no clue of the weeks of insomnia that sent me spiraling into depression, hopelessness, and in my darkest moments considered ending not just my marriage but my life as well. She doesn't deserve this meeting. I owe her nothing.

Inside, though, I feel it's the right thing to do. There is a stirring within me. Perhaps I'm ready to move on, to let go of the hurt and the anger?

So I drive. And I breathe. Without realizing it I begin to recite the Buddha's lovingkindness meditation.

May I be safe.

May I be happy.

May I be healthy.

May I live with ease.

I repeat this the entire twenty minute drive. First for me. Then for my kids, who are still hurting. Finally, I repeat it for the mistress. Yes, even for this woman who was a part of destroying my family.

It's obvious she is as nervous as I am. So I sit quietly, just listening. There is power in silence. The quieter I am the more she talks. She tells me very little that shocks me and confirms much of what I had suspected. The more she speaks the more I begin to see the truth.

This is a woman who is also hurting.

Yes, she was part of a decision that ruined my family. Yes, she is culpable and must live with her decisions. But, sitting in front of me is a woman with her own demons to wrestle with. I can scream and curse at her. I can cut her with my words. She is sitting close enough I can reach out and strike her physically.

I choose not to.

Hurting her will not help me heal. If my yoga and meditation practice have taught me anything it's that it is not about her. It's about me.

No matter how fledgling my yoga practice has been lately, if I am to truly practice yoga I must also remember to take what I have learned on the mat and to apply it to my life off the mat.

I choose to practice ahimsa. Ahimsa is more than just a lack of violence. Obviously I shouldn't physically harm people, no matter how much pain they have caused me. But ahimsa also means thoughtful consideration of other people. Although her karma is hers to deal with and my karma is mine, I can still acknowledge that she, too, is a woman awash in torment.

When choosing my words I choose satya. Yes, I am speaking the truth, but I am speaking in a way as to not cause further harm to anyone else.

As we get up to leave from our meeting I look one more time at this woman. I don't anticipate sharing lattes with her any time soon. But I realize the universe has used her to teach me that no matter what negative choices she was a part of, I can choose to start living again. I can release the negativity that I have been holding on to. It no longer serves me.

Compassion has allowed me the privilege of finding happiness again.

* Previously published Elephant Journal May 6, 2013

Surrender and Santosha

Surrender doesn't mean to give up. It means to cease resistance, to end your war with reality. Accept 'life is perfect' exactly as it is right now.

Notice I didn't say your life is as you want it to be. Or your life is how you think it should be or how you feel you deserve it to be. Life, at this moment, is exactly as it should be.

You may be looking around right now and thinking 'Who

am I kidding? You have kids running wild, not enough money to pay the rent, a husband who refuses to be your partner and an ill parent to care for'. This is not your idea of a perfect life!

No, it's not. Neither you nor your life are perfect. But both you and your life are perfectly designed. Surrender is raising your hands, turning your eyes upward, and saying "Thy will be done."

Please, dear God, thy will be done because I sure can't do this anymore. I no longer have the energy or the strength to control what goes on around me. And, truth be told, my control issues haven't served me all that well anyway.

During one of my early meetings with my life coach she told me I was addicted to control. Gee, you think? I have six kids, a full-time job and an alcoholic husband. You bet I'm doing my damn best to control the chaos around me.

My mom would always fly down to wherever I was living to watch the kids when I went out of town for yoga teacher trainings. I'd spend the whole week prior to leaving filling the freezer with ready-to-eat healthy meals, doing all the laundry and writing out pages of notes for daily routines, bedtimes, school information, and even reminders to feed the dogs. My mom raised two children herself. This wasn't her first rodeo. Yet even when away from home I needed to be in control. All this controlling earned me the nickname 'Puppet Master.'

It was all an illusion. I see now that I was and am now no more in control of those around me than I can control what time the sun rises. My addiction to control was an impractical and ineffective way to own my power. I didn't have the confidence to stand up to the chaos around me and say no more. I will no longer accept being treated in a way that does not respect or elevate me. Instead, I did all I could to force my power on those around me by controlling the little things and ignoring the big things spiraling just outside my grasp.

The second Niyama of Patanjali's Eight Limbs is santosha, meaning contentment, to be content enough to relinquish control and have reverence for a bigger, Universal authority.

Santosha is no longer going after the illusion of a perfect family and perfect life. Contentment is not filling your life with external materialistic possessions in hopes of feeling better about yourself or appearing more important to those around you. Santosha is looking at what you already have and being grateful and appreciative, knowing that if you are meant to have more or different, it will appear when the time is right.

Learning to surrender will at first take as much energy as enforcing control. However, it's a much less frenetic and more peaceful energy with much longer lasting results.

Once you are willing to surrender your control to a higher power, you are ready to accept what is. But, let me be very clear, acceptance is not the same thing as condoning. It is never acceptable to condone the behavior of someone who intentionally hurts or harms you. You do not have to be anyone's doormat. You don't own your power when you allow someone elses behavior to continue to hurt you, either physically, emotionally or spiritually.

Acceptance is seeing the situation for what it is. Acceptance is loving the sinner, but not the sin. Once I finally surrendered my power to stop my husband's drinking and accepted that he was fighting his own battle I took back my power and began to live my own life again. By owning my power and standing strong in my choices, the situation didn't become bigger than me and I was more peaceful and happy.

By accepting the unacceptable, I removed the angst and negative energy that was consuming me. Once the negative energy was gone, I freed up space for a more positive energy to flow. I allowed myself to be happy again with myself and my life.

By contentment, supreme joy is gained.

Yoga Sutra 2:42

It is possible to find joy in an unpleasant situation. First, release the anger and guilt, surrender your control (or lack thereof), and finally, accept that it is indeed an unpleasant situation.

When my mom was dying of cancer I was very angry. She was only 62 and entirely too young to be so sick. I was also dealing with a lot of guilt because I lived so far away and my sister had the sole burden of taking on the extra responsibilities. And I was angry at the doctors. The night before my mom was diagnosed with liver, lung, and brain cancer, she had attended a tai chi class and walked her dog. She wasn't sick. Not until she began the chemotherapy did my mom become an old and sickly woman. I was mad at her doctors because in my eyes the treatment they were giving her was what was destroying her.

On one of my visits home my anger came erupting out at her oncologist. We were sitting in the exam room as the doctor explained mom needed to decide to either discontinue treatment or try one more round of chemo. I couldn't take the heaviness anymore and I screamed at her doctor, "She wasn't sick and old until she started your chemo treatments!" The doctor calmly looked at me and said she'd be dead by now if she hadn't had chemo.

Dead.

The word stopped me. I didn't know what to say. I'm not even sure I remembered how to breathe. My mom turned to me and very gently said, "Jennifer, it's time to accept I'm going to die."

At the moment my anger at the situation began to fade. This was going to happen and even I, the Puppet Master, couldn't prevent it. After that doctor visit we joined my sister for lunch at our favorite restaurant. I don't remember what we ate, but I remember how we laughed. We made horribly inappropriate jokes, we retold funny stories and we laughed so hard we drew the stares of other diners around us.

My mom was dying, yet at that moment we were living a joyful life.

VIKRAM

What are you guilty of?

Has anyone besides yourself judged you guilty?

Is anyone besides yourself punishing you?

Make a list of the ways your guilt is holding you back from going after what you want.

Are you willing to practice ahimsa, release your guilt and stop punishing yourself?

Whom are you angry with? Why?

Is it possible you are really angry with yourself? Spend some quiet time reflecting on the anger you hold in, and how it manifests physically, emotionally, and spiritually.

Are you willing to forgive those around you? Are you wiling to forgive yourself?

What does that forgiveness look like?

What reality are you fighting right now? How would accepting your reality change your life?

Are you willing to practice santosha in order to find inner peace? Write a note or draw a picture of what manifesting peace in your life would look like.

In what ways can you stand strong in your own power without trying to control the actions of those around you?

MEDITATION MOMENT

Simhasana

Lion's Breath

Meditation doesn't necessarily have to be quiet and serene. Sometimes a good shout is what we need to let off steam and return to a quieter, calmer place.

In yoga, we use a technique called Lion's Breath. Let me just tell you upfront, you look a little silly and you will feel a little silly at first. But you've probably tried other ways to relieve stress that haven't been successful, so why not try something a little different today.

Find a quiet, comfortable place where you are alone and won't be disturbed. Sit on your knees, placing a yoga bolster or pillows under you for support. Be sure you use enough pillows to be comfortable on your knees and ankles. Of course if sitting this way isn't accessible to you, just find a comfortable place to sit.

Bring your hands to your knees, fingers splayed wide, sit tall and close your eyes. Become aware of your breath inhaling through your nose and exhaling through your nose. Notice if the breath is smooth and even, or is it forced and shallow? Begin to even out your breath, allowing your body to soften.

As you exhale, imagine you are releasing pent up anger, frustrations, hurt, and disappointment. As you inhale, bring in pure, cleansing breath to fill the space left empty by the released negativity.

Take a few rounds here silently. When ready, open your eyes and focus on a spot in front of your nose. Lean forward, open your mouth wide and stretch your tongue down toward your chin. Roar a giant exhale out of your mouth. Allow your breath to make a "HA" sound as it passes over the back of your throat.

Inhale through your nose cleansing, light air and then once again lean forward and roar your exhale. Repeat three times or as many times as needed.

When you are finished roaring sit back and take a few regular cleansing breaths. Notice if you feel a little calmer, or at least a little lighter.

Allow yourself to carry this lighter presence with you through the rest of your day. Give yourself permission any time you feel the negativity creeping back in to return to Simhasana and roar your way to peacefulness again.

AFFIRMATION

I accept responsibility for what is mine and I am willing to release what I do not own.

I invite contentment and peace into my life.

I have room in my life for joy and happiness.

YOUR PERSONAL NOTES

5

BE ADAPTABLE

"We must be willing to get rid of the life we planned, so as to have the life that is waiting for us."

Joseph Campbell

My husband had a 23-year career in the US Navy, which meant every few years he would uproot me and our increasing number of children to move to another state and a new duty station. He, of course, would settle in right away to his new Navy job, while the kids and I struggled to take care of the important things, make new friends, adjust to new schools, find new doctors and new hair dressers that we liked. It was an exciting life, but at times a difficult life being separated from family over the holidays and during family milestones.

Although we were fortunate to be able to spend a few years at a Navy base in my hometown, as we knew would happen, once again it was time to move on.

With the van packed and the kids in their car seats, I leaned out the car window to say one last goodbye to my mom. As we pulled away, she placed a piece of paper into my hand. As my husband drove down the road, I unfolded the paper and read: Bloom Where You Are Planted.

Even non-military families don't always get to decide where they will live, what job will support their home or how close to family they will be. As a Northern city girl, I never would have imagined living in the rural South for as long as I have. And, I admit, I have spent more than a considerable amount of time whining and complaining over having to live in a place I didn't want to be.

Yet here I am. I have done my best to bloom in this unfamiliar Southern soil I've been planted in. And there you are. You have a choice to make. Will you bloom? Or refuse to put down roots and die?

Remember, you are exactly where you should be at this moment at this time. Look around, notice where you are needed. Let your spirit fulfill its fate here.

The Universe Doesn't Negotiate With Complainers*

"Why am I stuck here?" I shouted out to the Universe.

"Because this is where you are needed," She whispered back.

It wasn't the answer I expected. Nor the answer I wanted.

Surely there must be a need somewhere else? Maybe somewhere with a beach?

I had just returned from an enchanting week in Los Angeles where I had the opportunity to study with my yoga teacher, get my feet wet in the sand, and drink Kombucha while watching the sunset. That lifestyle, even if it was just a mini-working vacation, can be intoxicating.

I spent the first few days back home here in rural Tennessee stomping my feet and complaining about the lack of vegetarian options, oppressive humidity, and just plain old un-hip lifestyle.

My weekly yoga class for teen ballerinas forced me to take a temporary break from my incessant complaining. Halfway through class one of the young girls was struggling and tears began to fill her eyes. Instinctively, I knelt next to her and together we got through the series of poses.

'This is where you are needed.'

I swear I heard it as if someone in the room had said it. Can't we negotiate this where I'm needed thing? Like, maybe somewhere with a beach?

Damn, I guess when you ask the Universe a question you have to be willing to accept the answer.

In his book *The Wisdom of Yoga*, Stephen Cope says as humans we wage a silent War With Reality inside ourselves. The ancient yogis called it dukha, which translates to suffering or distress. Thoreau called it a 'life of quiet desperation'. In modern times, even us practicing yogis find ourselves in deep aversion to how things are right now.

I want to be there.

I don't want to be here.

As Cope points out, there is a direct connection between my dukha and my inability to perceive reality accurately. Each time I complained about having to suffer and live here I reinforced the samskaras, those deeply-rooted patterns in my brain that said, "Yeah, you're right. It really must suck living somewhere you have a roof over your head, a family that loves you, and a job that fulfills you."

Damn you, Universe! Can't I just wallow a little longer while I adjust to the time zone?

So, what's a good yogi to do to stop the negative patterns?

Meditate, of course.

Cope says one of the first lessons a new meditator must learn is "we are not our thoughts. We are not our internal chatter."

So if I think I'm stuck here, then I'm stuck here. But Patanjali says "Things outside neither bind nor liberate you; only your attitude toward them does that."

With meditation, awareness, compassion and a great big attitude adjustment, Cope says everyone can break those old samskaras that say I won't want this but I do want that.

I accept the Universe has placed me here now for a reason. And I accept it may be a reason I'm not supposed to know. But I am totally open to the Universe at some point, I hope soon, needing me someplace else.

Someplace with a beach.

*Previously published Elephant Journal August 2011

Are you waging a war with your current reality? Take a look around at the source of your suffering. Are you choosing to suffer? It is a choice.

Think Global, Act Local

When I first moved to Tennessee, no yoga classes were offered within an hour's drive of where I lived. Once I started teaching my classes were very small at first, often just a couple people. Yoga was something that this community hadn't had much exposure to and it took time build a reputation for myself as a teacher, and time to build a now still-growing yoga community in my rural area.

I sometimes envy those who teach in a big city fancy yoga studio with complimentary hot tea, posh changing rooms and an organic café next door. My classes are taught at local gyms, recreation centers and even church basements. But the reality is, I love it!

My students know when they show up they will probably have to push tables and chairs out of the way. There aren't enough props for everyone so we gladly share the few yoga blocks and straps with each other. My students don't look like the yogis featured in yoga videos or fitness shows. We're just a bunch of average people gathering together once a week to move a little, breathe a little, and find an hour of peace in an otherwise hectic life.

I make no promises that if a big-time yoga magazine or a swanky New York City yoga studio calls me up I won't be tempted take the offer. Actually, I'm pretty sure as much as I'd be flattered I'd stay right where I am. I am filling a need where I am now. And that is what fulfills me and contributes to my purpose every day.

What is it you would love to have the opportunity to do? Take a look around you now. How can you do what you love where you are?

Before children, I wrote for local newspapers. When the babies started coming I continued to do some small magazine writing, but eventually breastfeeding, diaper changing and daily drudgery became too much to form a complete sentence. I begrudgingly put my writing aside. At times, as depression and hopelessness took over, I convinced myself I'd never write again. Once again, I had believed my own lies.

Looking back though, I can see how I did find a way to keep writing. No matter what group I was a part of, I was always in charge of writing or editing the newsletter. If the group didn't have a newsletter, I created one!

Unfortunately, at the time I didn't see that my newsletter writing had value. I would say things to myself like " I don't do any 'real' writing anymore." I was building new negative samskaras telling myself that my life and my work had no value.

It was, of course, my mom who reminded me I had a gift. I was putting words on paper and people were reading them. I was fulfilling a need for my local group. That was real and that was valuable.

Recently I received a Facebook message from a woman who had been in a young mothers group I had written the newsletter for many years ago. She said she was glad to reconnect again and thanked me for a piece of my writing from so long ago. She said she kept my column hanging on her refrigerator for years before finally passing it on to another young mom who needed to read it.

Of course, I was honored and touched that something I wrote meant enough to her to keep for so long. But the most amazing part of this story? I don't even remember writing the article.

Never diminish the contributions you make in your own backyard.

"Where your talent meets the needs of the world, there lies your calling."

■ *Aristotle*

Follow Your Bliss

Growing up, I wasn't really sure what I wanted to do with my life. And, to be totally honest, in my twenties and thirties I still wasn't totally sure what I wanted my life to be. I knew I wanted to write. I wanted to teach. And I wanted to travel.

Once I hit my forties it all suddenly came together. Well, not really suddenly. I had spent years laying the groundwork, paying my dues, studying myself and at times wandering aimlessly on what seemed like a path to nowhere. In fact, the path led to this place right here.

I teach yoga, I write and I've been fortunate enough to travel for both my yoga and the writing. I couldn't have planned this life if I tried.

One of my mom's favorite sayings was follow your bliss. I remember when I was just beginning my undergraduate work in journalism I told my mom I wasn't sure this was the most logical major for me because writers don't make a lot of money. 'Just follow your bliss and the money will come', she told me.

Years later, when I thought my writing career was gone forever and I was beginning to train as a yoga teacher, again I was concerned about the financial stress training for a new career would bring to my family. And once again, I was picking a career not known to provide an abundance of money to make a living.

Mom's advice was the same: follow your bliss.

I can't sit here and say the money is rolling in. I just completed this year's taxes so I have paper proof that I have not chosen careers that have paid off in financial windfalls.

However, I am living abundantly. I love what I do. I am one of the fortunate ones who doesn't dread going to work in the morning. I have all that I need and most of what I want.

I also know I have been blessed to live in a situation that allows me to follow my bliss. If you are a single mom reading this, or the sole breadwinner in your house, you might think 'follow your bliss' is a luxury you can't afford. The truth is, you can't afford not to.

Like most other middle aged women faced with a sudden and unexpected divorce, there came a time when I had to put on my big girl panties and find a full-time job to help support me and my six children. At first I was mad, then scared, then hopeless that I'd have to work a job I hate. How would writing, yoga, and traveling be possible now that I was solely responsible for the care and financial needs of six children?

How? All the work I had done previously allowed the Universe to come together and provide me with a full time job still in the fitness field, with enough flexibility to care for my kids, and if I was really careful about pinching pennies, there might be just enough money to afford a little bit of yoga and travel. It's not exactly the life I had envisioned, but I still get to follow my bliss.

I'm not rich. But I am happy.

What is it you enjoy doing? First, decide what makes you happy. Then find a way to incorporate that into your life.

Natalie works for the court system. It's not a creative job, nor a lucrative job, but one she excels at and allows her to provide for her three children, one with special needs. Working in immigration court Natalie sees a lot of hardship and families being separated. By her own admission, some days it wears her down and leaves her spirit empty. Because her job doesn't offer health insurance, she has the additional financial stress of caring for her own health issues.

Natalie finds her bliss in making jewelry. The color, texture, and shape of the beads excite her. When I asked her to make a set of Mala Beads for me, the only requirements I had were earthy tones. The results were breathtaking. Exactly what I wanted even though I never could have designed it myself. Custom designing jewelry allows Natalie to set her creativity free and let her spirit soar. It's her bliss.

On weekends Natalie sells her jewelry at local craft shows and markets. It's not making her wealthy financially, but crafting jewelry enriches Natalie's creative soul.

Finding your dharma

When my husband proposed to me I said, 'Okay. but I'm going to finish college, have my own career and we're not having any children'. After that kind of response it's surprising the guy even wanted to still marry me! But I had a plan and I wasn't going to deviate from that plan.

Woody Allen said, "If you want to make God laugh tell him about your plans." God must have been rolling on the floor laughing the day I said yes to a marriage but with conditions.

I had no idea how much my plans would change on that day so long ago, sitting in the park with my to-be husband down on one knee. Thank God I didn't. Even now, after much disappointment and divorce, I'm still glad I said yes. Otherwise, I would have missed out on some amazing moments.

I recently mentioned to a friend that in another life I'd be a photojournalist taking Pulitzer Prize winning photos in the middle of the latest war zone. I have no plans to ditch my current life and run away. But, there was a time when I thought that would be my life.

Although the bulk of my picture taking now is kids and dogs, I still harbor a love for photojournalism. I don't have an artistic eye for lighting or glamour, but I knew when to snap to capture a moment in time that spoke a story words couldn't tell.

But, like most stories, mine took a different turn. I met my husband, moved with his career, had babies, and made a different life. It's not a bad life. Just a different life than I once planned.

The only part that saddens me about my unplanned path is I no longer have my photography portfolio anymore. In a moment of postpartum depression I threw it away. I didn't lose it in one of our many moves. It didn't get destroyed by Hurricane Katrina. No, I picked it up out of the closet, walked it down to the end of our street and threw it into the dumpster.

Yet another example in my life of never make a major decision when you are over tired and in the throes depression. Convinced I'd never do anything again beyond changing diapers and breastfeeding, I couldn't see my life's path wasn't permanently blocked, it was only temporarily detoured.

Instead of standing strong I was letting my life define me. I believed the samskaras that told me I was just a mom and no longer a productive, creative member of society. In fact, they became a self-fulfilling prophecy. It would be years before I would pick up a camera or take pen to paper again.

Although when I did once again begin taking pictures and writing, my goal was no longer to win a Pulitzer Prize. I was creating for myself only. I didn't care if anyone else liked or even looked at my work. It was created for me by me. I was owning my power and in turn finding my authentic self.

Art is meant to be shared, and eventually I had the self confidence to share my work with others. The more I let out the real me, the more people responded and the more writing opportunities came my way. I started a blog as my way of getting the crazy out. The blog got noticed and led to a permanent writing job with an internet magazine. That led to contacts with writers and publishers. And here I am now, writing a book.

My path wasn't as direct and hurdle free as I planned, but here I am, 23 years later, doing exactly what I wanted to do. My dharma, my purpose, is beginning to be revealed.

"The two most important days in your life are the day you are born, and the day you find out why."

-- Mark Twain

VIKRAM

What are you constantly complaining about in your life? Has complaining changed your life in any positive way?

In what ways has your life turned out the way you wanted? In what ways is it drastically different? Make a list of the differences. Be sure to note the positive things that have happened that you didn't plan or expect.

Are you willing to let go of the vision you had and embrace the life you have?

If you aren't willing to let go, what are you willing to do now to make that vision come true? What changes do you need to make?

What dreams have you given up on? Have you really given up or just put them on hold?

Write down what you want, and then list the steps you need to get there. Don't impose a timeline on achieving what you want.

Where is your bliss?

Take a look around at your community. There is a need there for you and your bliss. If you don't see it right away, look deeper. Tell everyone you meet what you're looking for, what you want to do.

Be open to each and every opportunity that presents itself to you. No matter how small, it has the potential to lead somewhere bigger.

MEDITATION MOMENT

Nadi Sodhana

Alternate Nostril Breathing

Nadi Sodhana, or alternate nostril breath, is another pranyama (breathing) practice used in yoga. Each day as you breathe normally, the breath alternates between the two nostrils with one side being dominant over the other. The dominant nostril usually switches about every two hours.

Nadi Sodhana improves brain function by making sure each half of the brain is functioning equally. It also is excellent to increase mental clarity, increase oxygen intake and calm the mind and nervous system. I've found it very useful to help with allergy or sinus issues as well.

To begin, find a comfortable, quiet place to sit. Use pillows, blankets or bolsters as needed to prop your body to be comfortable and relaxed. You might want to have a tissue nearby in case your sinuses begin to clear and drain.

Place your right thumb over your right nostril and inhale through the left side of your nose. Rather than forcibly inhale, try to breathe in to a slow count of three. Now close the left side of your nostril with your right ring finger and open and exhale through the right side of your nose. Exhale to at least a slow count of three, perhaps even longer. This is half a round of Nadi Sodhana.

Keeping the left side closed, inhale through the right nostril to a slow count of three. Using your thumb, close the right side, open and exhale through the left nostril to a slow count of three or more. This completes one full round of Nadi Sodhana.

Aim for three complete rounds to begin. When finished with the pranyama, bring your wrists to your knees and close your eyes. Notice the state of relaxation of your body. Now that your mind is clearer and more focused, allow any thoughts or ideas to emerge. Imagine your thoughts are a movie, you are aware of them, but not actually a part of the thoughts.

If an idea or solution emerges, perhaps you will want to quietly jot down a quick note to refer to later. Don't get caught up though in trying to make sense of what your mind is showing you. What you are meant to know will always return to you when needed.

Sit here quietly as long as possible. When ready, bring your hands together in front of your heart. Inhale and exhale one final big full breath through your nose. Allow this light, peaceful feeling to carry you through the rest of your day and until you return to your meditation spot again.

AFFIRMATION

I am living a purposeful and valuable life. My life has meaning. I seek out opportunities to make a positive difference.

YOUR PERSONAL NOTES

6

BUILDING YOUR TRIBE

We aren't meant to go through life alone. Our joy and happiness and even our struggles and sadness are meant to be shared with those we love and those who love us. When I am going through a difficult time, I get very quiet and begin to isolate myself. The only thing this has ever accomplished is making me feel like I really am alone.

Satsang is a Sanskrit word for being in the company of the wise. Those closest to me know that if I've gone quiet, something is wrong. They are wise when I am being foolish.

The importance of other women in your life can't be stressed enough. Other women are the rock that we hold on to when we feel like we are drowning. They are the ones who insist we celebrate even the smallest of our accomplishments. And other women keep us accountable to being our own best woman we can be.

The women I surround myself with are my friends, my sisters, my tribe. They are not my bitches or my hos as in the way I so often hear younger women refer to each other. Does this mean I'm middle aged and no longer cool? Perhaps.

I prefer to surround myself with like-minded women who will uplift me. Those who will hold me to a higher standard. Those who will put me on the pedestal that I as a Goddess deserve, not tear me down with slang terms and derogatory names.

I will not call my friends those names and they know not to

call me those names. They are my sisters. They know that words have power.

I do not allow anyone to call me derogatory names. My daughters will not allow anyone to use those ugly labels around them. My sons know they are never to use those terms when referring to or speaking about or to a woman. Women are worth more. I am worth more.

Allowing someone, anyone, to call me one of those names doesn't diminish the power of the word, it diminishes the power of me.

It is not possible to stand strong while allowing someone else to push you down. The job of my female friends is to uplift and support me. As I feel responsible to uplift and support them.

MY STARBUCKS KULA

I was teaching my regular Wednesday morning yoga class when I noticed one of my long-time students and friends was really struggling. Shauna said every time she stood up she got dizzy.

"Hey, maybe you're pregnant!" I joked. By the look on her face I knew this was no laughing matter.

After class as the rest of our regular group gathered around, she told us not only was she dizzy, but she'd also been nauseated and extremely tired for over a week. Oh, no. This had potential to not be a happy moment.

Shauna had just enrolled her three children into public school after homeschooling for the past seven years. She herself was in her last year of nursing school and overwhelmed with studying, paperwork and trying to still be a wife and mother. A new baby would not be a welcome addition to her life right now.

As Shauna and the rest of our group left to talk some more, I stayed behind to get ready to teach my next class. Within the hour I got a text message: She's negative!

Wait a minute. I thought my friends were going to talk some more. Did Shauna take a pregnancy test already? Yes, she sure did. I texted back my relief and congratulations, but had to ask, "Are you at Starbucks?"

Yes, indeed, while her friends stood guard at the door, Shauna took a pregnancy test in the bathroom of Starbucks. As soon as my last class was finished, I met my friends there for a quick celebration and a good laugh.

Only real friends will wait for you to pee on a stick in a public bathroom!

The friends I have met teaching and practicing yoga have become my kula, my family. In Sanskrit kula can be translated as a grouping together or a place where you put your heart. We practice yoga together, we laugh together and we cry together. They have my heart and I have theirs. Our energy is united in a positive, successful life for each other.

Years ago, when I felt my life was spiraling down, I surrounded myself with people who agreed my life was a hot mess. Rather than try to find a way out of the current misery, my gathering with these women was always the same complaint session. Life isn't fair. I'm so unhappy. It's not my fault.

Not only were these conversations not productive, they did nothing to encourage me to do better. They did not help me be better. My social circle during that time only reinforced the negative samskaras I had already developed.

Were these women not my real friends? Perhaps. Or more likely they were women feeling as stuck and out of control as I felt. None of us were able to take the first step toward creating a joyful life, none of us even knew what that first step was.

When you know better, you do better.

My current kula still has its fair share of complaint time. But now it's different. Now we hold each other accountable. Yes, this is a difficult time you are going through. 'What are you going to do about it?' we ask each other. And, how can I help? We are not brutally honest with each other. Rather we are love-based honest with each other. We speak the truth, a truth based in kindness and love.

The friendships you have now in the good times are building the foundation for later when the bad times come. I realized the truth of this when my husband walked out on me and our children.

When I first found out about the break up of my marriage I hid. I stopped teaching classes. I stopped getting out of bed. I stopped answering the phone. I turned my back on my kula.

I was embarrassed. I was ashamed. I was hurt and confused. I was spiraling down faster than I ever had before. I needed help but couldn't bring myself to ask for it.

My friends knew something was wrong, very wrong. Finally one day they gave me no choice but to talk to them. And through tears it all came tumbling out. There's another woman, he's gone, it's over, I'm all alone.

They gathered me in their arms and told me I am absolutely not alone. My pain is their pain and together we will figure this out. Through phone calls, text messages, and regular tear-filled Starbucks meetings, they got me through those initial trauma filled first few weeks, filing legal papers and finally the divorce.

They held me when I was hurt, loved me when I felt unloved, reminded me my life was crazy but I was not, and celebrated with me as I found myself again.

A satsang is strengthened when it comes to the aid of a weaker member. Although friendships may fade with time and distance, the bonds are never really broken.

My mom lived in the same house for almost 40 years. She raised her children with a street full of other young mothers all dealing with the same issues. Their friendships moved through many different phases as their lives changed from raising young children, to teenagers, to empty nesters to starting new careers themselves.

I doubt that the day my mom moved into her house with her young family that she realized she was starting her own satsang. Through good and bad, and even at the end, Mom's satsang was there for her.

From my blog entry dated January 27, 2011:

Last night's Thunder Snow dropped sixteen inches of very heavy, very wet snow upon my area. When I woke up this morning it was beautiful. The trees were bending almost in half under the weight of the snow. It was pure white everywhere you looked.

But there was little time to enjoy it. We needed my parent's road and parking area cleared so the ambulance could transport mom to inpatient hospice. She needed to get there. It was time.

My two nephews, ten and sixteen, were outside even before me to begin shoveling. At first I just stood there, overwhelmed by the sheer magnitude of where to begin.

"Just start shoveling!", the ten year old hollered at me.

Sixteen new fresh inches on top of the six inches already on the ground from last weeks storm. Where do we dump our over-full shovels?

The mounds of snow we cleared lining the sidewalk and parking lot are almost as tall I am.

As we were working up a sweat in the cold temperatures, the neighbors began drifting out to see for themselves. One of the men on the street told me not to bother, that once the plow came down the street we'd have to start all over again anyway.

No, we have to keep shoveling. We need to get Mom out.

Soon word began to spread, and almost the whole street was out shoveling with us. At one point we realized the snowplow wasn't coming because our street was literally snowed in. No one could get in or out past the huge snow drifts that were blocking the way.

So little by little, shovel by shovel, we moved the snow.

The ambulance arrived right on schedule and immediately got stuck on one small patch we thought was out of the way. The neighbors didn't need told what to do. Everyone immediately started shoveling and throwing salt under the ambulance's tires to make it easier to drive.

And then the neighbors disappeared. I don't know if the task was done so they moved on, or if they left to let Mom preserve her last bit of dignity as she was wheeled out of her home for the last time.

But her path was prepared with the love of the neighborhood she lived in for almost forty years. The kids that I played with as a child, that she was room mother to a long time ago, are now adults living here. They, and their children, helped clear the way for her.

My nephew left before the ambulance wheeled mom out. He couldn't watch. That's okay. His final gift to her was complete.

We'd all done everything we could to make mom's transition as smooth and pain free as possible. I don't know of any other way her community could have said 'I love you'.

SEVA: SELFLESS SERVICE

Friendships are about more than just meeting for coffee or going to yoga class together. They help us get our needs met. Yet, the only way we ever really get our own needs met is by first helping others to get their needs met. Just like the preschool playground, to have a friend you first have to be a friend.

Years ago I belonged to a Mothers of Preschoolers (MOPS) group. With my natural controlling, need-to-be in charge tendencies I eventually wound up the coordinator of my group. My job, all volunteer of course, was the most visible but hardly the most important.

Any woman in the group who had the desire to serve had a place to serve. Whether it was helping in childcare, refreshments, scheduling speakers, or setting up the room, the group only worked because of the selfless service of the women in the group.

In the midst of my duties as coordinator, I noticed an interesting phenomenon. Every year, without exception, in the midst of all the new women who joined the group, there would be one woman who always sat in the corner and kept to herself. She was quiet, didn't seem to have any friends, and often presented an aura of unhappiness. She was probably deep in a downward spiral of negative samskaras that had her convinced her life was worth nothing more than changing diapers and doing laundry. Yet every week she would show up and sit in the back. I quickly learned that was the woman who most needed to find a place to serve.

Wendy was one of those women.

I asked Wendy if she would be willing to occasionally send out a note of encouragement to the other women in the group. Everyone likes to get mail, and few of us often get an unexpected "I'm thinking of you" type card, so I thought this would be a simple job that might just bring a smile to someone's face and let Wendy feel more a part of the group. I had no idea what was about to happen.

Even though Wendy was quiet and often kept to herself, she was definitely listening and paying attention when the other women spoke. Pretty soon, cards began to arrive in mailboxes regularly. When a mom was having marriage troubles, a note of encouragement showed up to remind her how strong she was. When a mom hadn't left the house in a week because she was busy caring for multiple kids all with the stomach flu, Wendy would show up with an emergency meal delivery and bouquet of flowers to brighten up the mom's day.

Those small notes and acts of service reminded the women that they were more than 'just a mom' and more importantly that they weren't alone. When an encouraging card arrived in the mail on a bad day, women were reminded to stand strong and not lose themselves. Wendy once again found purpose in her life. Her new-found confidence allowed her to stand strong and find the real Wendy, who had been buried for too long. Wendy had a gift with words and always knew exactly the right thing to say when someone was hurting. Friendships were formed while disappointments and celebrations were shared

My current teaching schedule includes yoga and aerobics for senior citizens. Even though they no longer have the struggles of young moms, these elderly women still need the acknowledgment that they are important and valued. One woman in our group is in charge of the birthday calendar. She supplies the cards, decorates them with beautiful calligraphy and makes sure to remind me when it's a birthday day. Our group's birthday coordinator uses her time to fill the needs of our group. And we all benefit. The funny thing is, even if someone has missed classes for awhile, you can bet she will return on her birthday!

Sometimes a well-timed card is all it takes to cement your tribe, because no act of service is too small to be unappreciated.

FIND A TEACHER

Before the invention of yoga teacher training schools, fitness certifications and online learning, yoga was learned by one student from one teacher. The history and philosophy were handed down slowly over time as the student was ready. Lessons were taught, re-taught, and taught again until they were mastered. Only then could the student move on to the next lesson. Eventually the teacher deemed you ready, and you then carried the responsibility to teach, and teach someone else, what you had learned.

Teaching, whether yoga, life philosophy, or grade school history is an honor and a responsibility. What you know must be respected and you in turn must be trusted to share the knowledge with those who are willing and ready to learn.

I've been extremely fortunate to have had many wonderful teachers in my life. Since my husband's military career took us away from family, I often called my teachers my second mom. They were there to guide me when my mom was not. Looking back, I can see now that any time I was struggling, an older, wiser woman would enter my life to guide me.

"When the student is ready, the teacher will appear" – Buddha

When I was working with my life coach, I'd often ask her 'Where were you twenty years ago?' I asked why she didn't work with younger women just starting out in their life.

"Because they don't listen!" she told me.

How true that is. At my current job I am manager to a staff of mostly young women aged twenty to twenty four. I listen to their boy troubles, family troubles, and fears for their future. I play the role of boss, mom and friend.

Sometimes I can't help myself and I have to do more than just listen. "Listen to me!" I tell them. "This is a valuable life lesson. I know. I've been there!"

Sometimes they listen. Sometimes they pretend to listen. It's okay, they are young and they have to learn the lessons for themselves in their own way.

Looking back, I can now see times where teachers were there for me, but I wasn't ready for them. I turned away from good advice. I refused to listen to reason. I wasn't ready.

If you have turned your back on those who have tried to help you, forgive yourself. Most people only hear what they are ready to hear, and what already conforms to their beliefs about their current reality. When you are deep in the grip of negative samskaras, no one can convince you of the wonder and joy that is around you.

Until you are ready.

Even if right now you feel stuck in your life and unworthy of love, deep down, maybe deep deep down, you know the truth. Inside you is a spark of the divine, and when she will no longer be silenced, you will be ready to listen and learn.

In the Yoga Sutras, Patanjali says that although all knowledge is within us and we don't need to get it from external sources, we do need help to understand that knowledge.

You already know you are beautiful and loved and loving. You just need someone to teach you to believe it. When you are ready, your teacher will appear.

Where can you find a teacher? Look around you. Whom do you respect and admire? Begin by reaching out to those women. Even if they aren't the right teacher for you at that time, odds are they will lead you in the right direction.

Be open to finding your teachers wherever they appear, in the oddest places. I met a fabulous woman in the back of an old, badly in need of redecorating chiropractic office.

Right now you don't know what you don't know. Stay open and have faith that when you are ready, the perfect teacher will appear.

BE A TEACHER

When I was first debating writing this book, I received an email from one of my students:

"I think I was waiting for you to step into my life as a teacher. And you are a magnificent teacher, thank you."

Me? A Teacher? Yes, I'm a yoga teacher obviously. But is it possible I have life lessons to teach as well? As I meditated on this thought one day, I realized that if nothing else, the yoga lineage has taught me that the student has a responsibility to one day become the teacher.

The lessons are only learned when applied, and then passed along.

I'm not comfortable when a student calls me their guru, even if they do usually say it jokingly. I am not a guru. I'm just as flawed a human being as the next person. Instead I tell them I have walked a long path, and I'd be honored to be your guide as you walk your own path.

My words in this book are my story and my answers. You have to find your own answers somewhere in the midst of your own story. Hopefully what you read here will guide you and nudge you along the path to your own truth. Don't trust anyone who claims to be a guru. Trust yourself. Be your own guru.

Even, I, as the teacher still have lessons to learn. I don't often get the luxury of taking a yoga class for my own personal enjoyment, but when I do, I struggle to turn off my teacher brain

I might start out by looking around the room at the other yogis and wonder if the teacher up front sees the same misalignments that I see. Or I'll question to myself why the teacher is cuing a certain pose. During times like this, I have to stop and step back for a moment. I realize I'm stepping onto my mat with an already full cup of knowledge. But this is my time on the mat to learn and explore. I don't have to be the teacher right now. I have to empty my own cup first, in order to allow this teacher to fill it again. There is always more to learn. The more open I allow myself to be to other teachers, the better teacher I can be to my students.

A teacher is a teacher because they are called to be. There is honor and pleasure, but usually not material reward. The reward you get from teaching is knowing that you are part of a lineage of self-empowerment and enlightenment. You have played a small part in making someone's life better.

The teacher might be forgotten, but the teachings will always be remembered.

VIKRAM

What qualities do you look for in a friend?

Do you consider yourself a good friend?

Take a look at your social circle, how many would you consider a real friend?

Is there anyone you could call right now that will drop anything and come to your aid? Is there anyone you would return the favor for?

Do you feel safe sharing both your struggles and your dreams with your friends?

Do your friendships generally uplift you and encourage you?

Make a date with your friends or send a card for no other reason than to express your gratitude for their friendship.

Who has served as a teacher/mentor to you?

What was the most valuable lesson you learned from this person or people?

Do you currently have a mentor/teacher?

Are you currently mentoring/teaching anyone? What do you feel you can teach someone else?

What one most important lesson would you like to pass along to someone? Write it down and find a way to pass it along.

MEDITATION MOMENT

Love Yourself, Love Others

Find a quiet, comfortable place to sit. Support your body with pillows, blankets or bolsters as necessary in order to allow your body to relax.

Close your eyes and focus on your breath. The inhale naturally flows in your nose, down your body and out to your extremities. The exhale naturally pulls the breath back through your center, up your body and out your nose. There's no need to force your breath. It happens naturally.

When ready, think of yourself as your own best friend. Imagine sitting next to yourself, giving yourself a comforting hug. If this feels odd or causes your breath to shallow or quicken, back off and return to a smooth, deep, natural breathing pattern.

When ready, once again think of yourself as your own best friend. This time, give yourself a big congratulatory hug. See yourself as happy and proud.

Now see yourself sitting with those you call your friends. Embrace each of them, allowing them to envelop you in love and happiness.

Think of those you see on a regular daily basis but often don't give much time to. Imagine giving them a friendly smile or saying an encouraging word.

Notice any tension melting in your body. Perhaps a smile, or a feeling of warmth has come over your body.

When ready, bring your attention to someone in your life you have difficulty with. Keep your breath smooth and even. Imagine just sitting next to this person, looking at them. Give them the love and respect you gave your friends and they gave you. Imagine this person willingly and openly accepting your embrace.

Commit to carrying this peaceful feeling with you throughout the rest of your day and until you return to your meditation space again.

AFFIRMATION

I am open and willing to accept the lessons the Universe has to offer me. I am ready to embrace any teacher that enters my life. I am eager to share the knowledge I've gained with others.

YOUR PERSONAL NOTES

7

YOU DON'T NEED TO KNOW WHERE YOU'RE GOING. JUST GET MOVING

A friend was recently sharing with me her fear of staying in her emotionally abusive relationship. She said, "I know I need to find some peace in my life. But I don't even know what that looks like".

Do you need to know what the end looks like I asked her? Or do you need to just get moving?

I'm scared. I'm afraid of what I'll find out there, she told me.

The devil we know is friendlier than the devil we don't know. Leaving a bad relationship, a bad job or making any major life change is scary. Your life might be better. It might not. The only guarantee is it will be different. If what you are doing right now isn't working for you, then it's time to look for something different.

"Everything's going to be ok in the end.

If it's not ok, it's not the end."

Unknown

Smash the crystal ball

I spent a lot of years paralyzed by fear. Unhappy with myself and my situation, but too afraid to do anything about it. What if I divorced and ended up living on welfare? Or if I stayed married and stayed miserable? Why bother trying to restart my career when I didn't even know if I ever had any talent to begin with?

If I could just see how my story was going to end then I could relax. I'd at least know if I was doing the right thing or not. I used to be so annoyed when my mom would say that which doesn't kill us makes us stronger. Well which was it going to be? Would this kill me or strengthen me?

When I speak with a woman now struggling to figure out her life's path, I tell her, *First stop and take a deep breath. Then, congratulations, you've made it this far. Wait until you see what is yet to come!*

But, please, I beg of you. Stop searching for the crystal ball. And if you do find it, smash it. It's a huge burden that you just don't need in your life.

Do you really want to see the days ahead when you are so angry you dare to curse God? Do you want to see the nights ahead where you drop to your knees absolutely convinced you will die of a broken heart? Do you want to witness the pain your loved ones are going to go through as they get sick? Or the utter grief you'll suffer as their death overwhelms you?

Your children are going to disappoint you, scare, you and shock the hell out of you. You don't yet need to know the depths of hell you'll be willing to walk through to save them.

There will be times in your life when you will question

whether you can go on.

The good news is, not only will you get up off your knees and face another day, but there will be days of such joy and delight that you won't want them to end.

You are going to sing and dance with abandon. You are going to laugh until it hurts. The love you are going to give and receive will swell your heart to a size you never knew possible.

Not only will your wishes come true, but you'll find new dreams on a new path you never expected.

Your life is the worlds greatest rollercoaster. Get ready, it's going to be one hell of a ride!

There is a big difference in not knowing where you are going and staying stagnant. It's okay to not know what your life will look like in five years, ten years or even next year! In fact, none of us have any guarantees. It's not ok to sit and do nothing.

Doing the same thing the same way you've always done it guarantees you will get the same results you've always gotten. If you want something different, do something different.

Is what you are doing today going to get you where you want to be tomorrow? At the very least, let the choices you make today lead you to a different place than where you are right now.

GET UP AND CHANGE YOUR LIFE

When you are depressed and beat down doing almost anything can feel overwhelming. Have you ever found yourself ly ing on the couch watching a mindless television show you have no interest in? Yet you don't have the energy to get up and find the remote to change it? Your life doesn't come with a remote.

When you are ready to change your life you have to get up and get moving.

But how do you do that when you don't even have the energy to get off the couch? You get off the couch!

When contemplating a big change it's easy to get bogged down in the massiveness of it. We know the outcome we want but we don't know the path to get there. It's scary, so too often we quit before we begin. We believe the samskaras that tell us it's just not worth it to even try. We are paralyzed once again by our own fear.

Don't think ten steps ahead, think right here right now. Maybe you want to finish your college degree but you have no money for tuition, no childcare and you are currently working a full time job just to make the rent. It seems daunting. But step back a moment, take a breath and break it down.

This month the only thing you need to do is gather information on local colleges. Yes, I know you can't afford them, but right now that doesn't matter. You are only seeing what schools and programs look interesting to you. Take your time. You haven't finished your degree yet so there's no rush now. Browse the college catalogues when you have a free minute, even if that means while you are in the bathroom.

Next month you begin circling programs of study that interest you. Maybe even researching any prerequisites for those classes. Yes, I know you still can't afford it and don't have childcare, that's not your focus just yet. Now that you have an idea of what educational path you think you'd like, start sharing your plan with everyone. Why keep it a secret? Will someone laugh at your or tell you it can't be done? You now know this person is not in your life to uplift or encourage you, so their laughter and ridicule doesn't matter. You are stronger than anyone else's negativity. Your friends who are encouraging you will also help keep you accountable to following through.

You are about three months in now to beginning your new life. Go ahead, take the plunge and fill out the college application form. Although so far I've encouraged you to take your time, now I'm not. Don't let those papers sit there in a clutter on your counter. Make the commitment to yourself to fill them out and submit them. You don't have all the details worked out just yet, but there's no harm in making an official application to the college.

Congratulation! You got accepted! Don't panic! There's still time to figure out the rest of the details. If you're acceptance letter didn't come with financial aid forms, call the school and ask. College counselors want to help you find a way to get an education. It's their job to help you so you are not wasting their time. In fact, odds are they can point you in the direction of affordable childcare. Many college campuses now offer childcare staffed by early learning education students. And I promise there will be a college student in need of some extra cash in exchange for babysitting. If the child-care funds just aren't there for you, look around at all the people you've told about your plan to return to school and who have encouraged your plan. Can anyone there help you? Have you even asked them? People don't know what your needs are until you tell them. Most people want to help, they just need told how to help.

Ok, so maybe college isn't your dream. The point is that whatever you want to do is out there waiting for you. No obstacle on the path is insurmountable if you stay focused.

The goal is big, but the steps to get there are small. When my students are working on a challenging pose, I always take time during class to break it down. The pose may be advanced, but it takes a lot of smaller, more basic prep poses to get there.

No one walks into their first class and does a headstand in the middle of the room. No one gets up off the couch and runs a marathon. No one makes a major achievement without doing the work ahead of time. When you adequately prepare the body and the mind, anything is possible.

In yoga your drishti is where your gaze is directed in any pose. For example in most seated forward folds the gaze is directed toward the toes. From an anatomical standpoint, gazing in a specific direction helps keep our bodies in alignment. But remember your attention flows where your energy goes. In the yoga room, if my attention is on fixing my hair, my energy is no longer in the pose. In life, if my attention is on achieving my goal, all my energy will be focused on that goal. When our attention wanders, we are led further away from what we truly want. We become easily distracted and lose sight of the path we set out on. Any time you are unsure if you are staying focused or wandering, ask yourself: Is what you are doing today going to get you where you want to be tomorrow?

Life will distract you. Your job is to stay focused. Sri K Pattabhi Jois, an Ashtanga yoga master, would tell his students, "Do your practice and all is coming." It doesn't matter if getting yourself into a headstand takes six months or six years. Actually, it doesn't matter if you ever get into headstand. It's not about the pose. It's about the work. In a yoga class you can't force the pose. Forcing a pose, forcing anything, only creates friction and stress. Instead, take a deep breath and diligently go about your prep work. Allow your body to open and the pose to evolve. Not only will the final pose be sweeter and more enjoyable, but you will enjoy the process to get there much more than if you had groaned, grunted and sweated your way through it.

The Universe will only take a step forward to you after you first take a step toward it. Stay focused and do your practice. Your goal might happen soon, it might happen later. What you do every day matters more than what you do every once in awhile. Stay focused and do your practice.

"It's impossible," said pride.

"It's risky," said experience.

"It's pointless," said reason.

"Give it a try," whispered the heart.

Clear Your Path With Love

As wonderfully calm and serene as it sounds to just relax and allow your life to unfold around you, let's be honest, it's not always that easy. As I was writing this chapter, my day had been a difficult day for me. It was busy, but no busier than normal. I had been looking forward for the past week to the two hours I had carved out of my schedule in the evening to focus on my own creativity. And then my husband decided to go feed his demons. And I had no control over that.

And when I feel a loss of control I need to quick find a way to gain some control back. What's the easiest thing to control? My own personal choices. As my disappointment set in deeper, I decided my scheduled creative time was stupid and why even bother. I'm just going to forget about it and go get myself a big greasy, fattening dinner and wallow in my misery.

Now the irony is, my husband choosing to go drink in no way affected my creative time. The kids were already situated in their own activities and with my husband not home, I had even more quiet time to myself. What was really happening was those old negative samskaras were making an appearance. My husband doesn't deem me worthy on this night. Therefore, it must be true and I'm not worthy. So why bother taking care of myself or attempting to create a work of art. It's not worth it. I'm not worth it.

My enemy on this night wasn't my husband. My enemy wasn't another disappointment. My enemy was inside my own head. I was about to do something permanently stupid just because I was temporarily upset.

If I act the part of the martyr and don't take care of my needs, and no one else is around to witness my martyrdom, am I a martyr or just a fool? When those around me choose to disregard me, yet I continue to take care of myself, I win. I am standing strong in my power.

The goal of yoga is enlightenment. Enlightenment doesn't mean sitting on a mountaintop, surrounded by white light and knowing all the answers to life's questions. Rather, yoga is meant to lead the practitioner from suffering to freedom. To help you realize your Divine Nature.

I don't need to act crazy or abuse myself when life is uncertain and chaotic. I am on a path to enlightenment – sometimes an uncertain path – but it will be a path I forage with love. When I have a choice to make, I need to remember to ask myself is what I am doing today going to get me where I want to be tomorrow? Would throwing away my much coveted creative time and eating food I know will make me sick get me to a better place?

Absolutely not.

Set an intention and maintain it with grace and dignity. When you are on a path to enlightenment make sure it's a path built with love. Barreling your way through life, lashing out at those who hurt you and making decisions based in anger will not get you to a better place. You must believe that it is possible to soar without knocking others down and then act accordingly.

Will your trek to enlightenment be easy? No. Will you have obstacles and setbacks along the way. Yes. Can you overcome them? Absolutely.

Even thousands of years ago, Patanjali knew the path was going to be rough. In the Yoga Sutras he listed nine obstacles, called vikshepas, that yogis would encounter on their path to enlightenment; illness, listlessness, doubt, carelessness, laziness, cravings, inability to progress, delusion and instability in maintaining progress. Any of those sound familiar

Yep, they sound familiar to me too.

The vikshepas you deal with along the way to enlightenment have the opportunity to either derail you or make you stronger. It's your choice. If you are willing to throw away what you want because the obstacle seems too daunting, perhaps you need to ask yourself is this really what you want. If something is important to you, you will find a way to make it happen. If it isn't important to you, you'll find an excuse. Stop making excuses.

When you are sick and tired of being sick and tired you will be ready to make a change. Love yourself enough to believe you have the power and the energy to change your life.

Do small things with great love.

-- Mother Teresa

Don't Look Back

When I was in middle school I joined my local YMCA swim team. I was a good swimmer but not great. I went to every practice and tried my best at every swim meet. Yet I never won a race. I often started out in the lead, yet my hand never hit the wall first. Of course I was discouraged and didn't understand why my hard work wasn't paying off.

One day as I was anxious about an upcoming meet, my mom told me, "You can do this. Just don't look back." She pointed out that each time I turned my head out of the water for a breath I would look to see where the other swimmers were in the lanes next to me. Those precious few seconds of looking around were costing me the win. I was too concerned about everyone else's race to focus on my own.

Years later when I became friends with long distance runners, they taught me to always finish strong. No matter what happened in the race, no matter how bad your knees hurt or your heels are bleeding, keep your eyes straight ahead and finish strong.

Don't look back! No matter what the race or struggle is, you can't clearly see the path ahead of you if you are too busy looking behind you. What happened in the past is over and you can't change it. Last week's race can't be repeated. You can only focus on the race today.

Make the decision that you will never again go back to where you were. I wasn't really living when I was hopeless and depressed. No matter what happens in my current race, I will not go back to hopelessness again. I just won't.

Just like every soul has their own journey to take, everyone is running their own race. How the person next to you prepares is what is best for them. Their training may not be the best method for you. You keep your drishti strong, finish your race and be proud of how far you've come.

People may judge you or tell you that your training methods are all wrong. Is it working for you? Do you feel a sense of accomplishment? Are you in even a slightly better place today than you were yesterday? Just as you drown out the negative voices in your head, you can drown out the negative voices around you.

It is very freeing when you decide you no longer have anything to prove to anyone but yourself. Know what you know and do what you do. Stay focused, stand strong and take the time to celebrate even the smallest of your victories. Even if it's a just a party of one, you deserve it.

"Run when you can,

Walk when you have to,

Crawl if you must,

Just never give up."

-- Dean Karnazes

Embracing Your Dharma

So many of us have been moving through life bouncing from one event to another in a seeming random out of control way. We fail to see the bigger connect-the-dots picture that every person is interconnected in the most perfectly designed way.

Think of it like a box of pictures you have shoved in the back of your closet. It would be much easier if we could just pull down a perfectly constructed scrapbook tied with a pretty pink bow. We could then open the book and see the story of our life neatly placed together in a logical, sensible order. The answers we so desperately crave would be all right there for us to understand.

But we aren't necessarily meant to see the whole book just yet. We get the privilege of little snapshots as they happen. Our job is to enjoy the pictures and trust the book will eventually come together and be revealed.

You just have to have faith that the book will have a happy ending. Have faith. Have faith in something. Have faith in God, have faith in the design of the Universe and have faith in yourself. Have faith that one day your dharma, your purpose, will be revealed. It is never too late. You are never too far gone. Your dharma is there waiting for you when you are ready to embrace it.

Many cultures have their own version of a person's path being predetermined. Jeremiah 1:5 says, "Before I formed you in the womb I knew you, and before you were born I consecrated you." There are many Biblical references to a persons days being numbered: "…for all your days are written in my book," Psalm 139:15-16. The Jewish tradition also teaches Divine providence and that God is intimately involved in the unfolding of human history.

The Bhagavad Gita is an ancient Hindu scripture. Composed of 700 verses, is the conversation between Lord Krishna and Prince Arjuna before the start of the Kurukshetra War. Although trained as a warrior, Arjuna is confused and uncertain about battling against his own cousins and former teachers who command the opposing army. Throughout the story, Lord of the Universe Krishna tells Arjuna that his path has already been chosen. His dharma, like my dharma and your dharma, is righteous and meant to benefit others.

Arjuna can't not be a warrior any more than I can't not write or you can't do what you are naturally meant to do. Our dharma is what we were born, what we were Divinely created to do.

Or as it was explained to me, Plan A is my plan. Plan B is my back up plan. But Plan C is the Universe's plan. When you get out of your own way, when you stop the self sabatoge and negative beliefs, Plan C is there just waiting for you to come dancing along and embrace the life that has been waiting for you.

The journey to discover who you are begins with awareness. Awareness that maybe you are staying too long with your Plan A that obviously isn't working for you. Awareness that every action you take matters. Awareness that what you think matters. Awareness that although you are not alone in the world, you are solely responsible for your thoughts and actions.

Right now, this moment is an opportunity to open to awareness and embrace your life that has been waiting for you.

You can start again right now.

And now.

And now.

Your work is not to drag the world kicking and screaming into a new awareness. Your job is to simply do your work... Sacredly, Secretly, and Silently... and those with 'eyes to see and ears to hear' will respond.

- The Arcturians

VIKRAM

What answers are you hoping to find in your crystal ball? Are you willing to trust that they one day will be revealed?

Is there a big change, dream or goal you've been wanting to pursue but haven't?

Use your journal to write down the absolute worst case scenario that could happen if you went after what you want. How realistic is that worst-case scenario?

At a different sitting, journal what achieving your goals would look like and how it would change your life.

What excuses are you giving yourself for not going after what you want?

Which of the vikshepas do you most struggle with? Put a plan in action today to fight that vikshepa.

What gets in your way of doing your daily practice? What do you need to rearrange to make your practice a priority today?

What do you feel comes naturally to you? What can you not imagine yourself doing? Spend time either in meditation or journaling to consider whether this is your dharma.

Celebrate a victory. It doesn't matter how small, take time to congratulate yourself on standing strong today.

MEDITATION MOMENT

Moving Meditation

If possible find a quiet, comfortable outside space for this walking meditation. Walking meditations are traditionally done in a circle, but walking the perimeter of your backyard or even the layout of your house will be just as beneficial.

Walking barefoot on the sand is my favorite place to be. Since I don't live near the beach, and most people don't, walking barefoot on the grass, dirt, pebbles or even concrete is good too. If going outside isn't possible, remove your shoes and socks inside your home. Whatever spot you have chosen, make sure you have a clear space in front of you to move.

Begin by standing tall, palms together in front of your heart with your thumbs to your breast bone. Close your eyes. Take a big deep inhale through your nose, and exhale completely out of your mouth with a big sigh. Repeat two more times allowing your inhales and your exhaling sighs to become bigger.

Once again be quiet and allow your breath to find its own pattern. Notice the feel of the earth under your feet. Wiggle your toes, perhaps rock back and forth heel to toe. Take some time here to become grounded to not just the space you occupy this moment, but to your space in the Universe.

When ready, open your eyes and slowly begin walking. Make each step purposeful. Left foot. Right foot. Notice how your heel hits the ground first. The foot rolls forward onto the toes. Do you feel both the big toe and little toe hit the earth at the same time? Does the ground feel smooth? Rough? Cold? Warm? Damp?

Allow the movement of your feet to set your rhythm. Continue walking and breathing at whatever pace your body sets. You have no pre-planned destination or time limit. Simply inhale and exhale. Place one foot in front of the other and continue to move forward.

As distracting thoughts emerge, bring your awareness back to your breath and back to the feel of the ground under you. You are walking on a ground that is spinning through space, yet you are stable and strong.

Continue walking as long as you can, again with no destination or self-imposed time limit. When ready, once again stand still. Close your eyes, take a big inhale in and one last time a large sighing exhale out. Notice how you feel. Before opening your eyes, commit to this peaceful feeling with you throughout the rest of your day and until you return to your meditation space again.

AFFIRMATION

My life is moving forward on a positive and productive path. I trust my instincts to know what is the best path for me. Each learning opportunity is another stone paved towards my ultimate success.

YOUR PERSONAL NOTES

8

IF YOU'RE GOING TO EAT FUDGE, THEN EAT FUDGE!

Every year before Christmas I called my mom and asked her to send me the fudge recipe. Each year she would tell me to write it down. Mom's last Christmas before she died she sent me an email with the recipe and at the very top she wrote, "Don't try to reduce the fat or sugar. IF YOU'RE GOING TO EAT FUDGE… EAT FUDGE!"

It's the only year I kept the email she sent me with the recipe. Now I have my mom's reminder to once in awhile, forget the fat and the calories, forget the eat something green rule and just enjoy the sweet treat.

Where dukha is the suffering in our life, sukha is the sweet-ess. Sukha is the sound of a baby's laugh, a glass of wine with friends and the touch of your lover. Sukha is what makes life worth living, but only if we take the time to notice and appreciate it when it happens.

There is much suffering in the world, and perhaps much suffering in your life right now. Without the suffering we can't learn to appreciate the joy. The pain makes the sweetness that much sweeter.

Attitude is Everything

When my kids are grumbling about chores, my students are groaning in a yoga pose, or those around me are grumbling about their troubles, I remind them that attitude is everything. Make it a good one. You can choose to be happy or you can choose to be miserable. Either way, it is your choice.

Yes there are chores to be done, but you have a beautiful home to do them in. Yes this pose is difficult, but how lucky you are to have the resources to take this class. Yes your job is exhausting and the laundry is never done. But you have a job and your kids are healthy.

A popular Buddhist saying is "pain is inevitable but suffering is optional." Bad things will happen, our reaction to them is our choice between suffering or not.

Sure, sometimes things happen in life that make it hard to stay positive. Little things like toddler tantrums or slow check-out lines. Bigger things like costly car repairs or unemployment. And there will be times the worst imaginable will happen to you including the loss of a loved one.

But life goes on, and you shall go on if you choose to.

Despite all the dukha, the suffering, in your life it's vital to have an attitude of gratitude. Gratitude is essential not despite of the suffering, but because of the suffering.

Gratitude should happen beyond the Thanksgiving table. When you approach life from a place of gratitude you see how much sukha, how much sweetness and joy you really have. Each November I keep a gratitude journal. Each day for the month I list five things I am grateful for that day. Some days it's a stretch to remember to be grateful. Other days I could have listed 500 reasons. At the end of the month I look back and inevitably the same things pop up over and over again:

1. Laughter – If you can make me laugh you have won me over. And even in the midst of a lot of tears, there is still a lot of laughter.

2. Yoga – Well this one is probably pretty obvious. I've told people that yoga saved my life. Although it sounds quite melodramatic, it's true. I found yoga at a time when I was spiraling down and my life was breaking apart. Yoga helped me find me again.

3. Teachers – Who always enter my life exactly when I need them.

4. My family – I have six children and they make me absolutely nuts at time. But thank God they are all healthy, basically productive members of society. Chauffeuring them and cheering them on at their various and costly extracurricular activities takes up a lot of my time, yet it made my gratitude list more than a few times

5. Friends – They help me remember that no matter how dark things may seem, we are all in this together.

A gratitude journal is easy when times are basically good. But can you be grateful when the only life you've ever known is collapsing around you?

I wasn't sure. But as usual, a yogi friend challenged me to find out.

November 2012 I was not only beginning the legal divorce process, I was severely depressed and to top it off, about to undergo knee surgery. What can I possibly find to be grateful about?

It turns out, a lot.

As usual friends made the gratitude list almost daily. As did my children who were my rock and salvation on days I couldn't function.

On crutches and in constant physical and emotional pain, there was no way I could cook a traditional Thanksgiving dinner for my kids. No one in my house really likes turkey anyway, we all just eat the dinner to get to the pumpkin pie. So the kids came up with Pizza, Pie, and Popcorn Day. We ordered pizza, ate pumpkin pie and went to the movies together. Back then I was grateful for creative and understanding children. It will always be my most memorable Thanksgiving.

Looking back over my journal from that time I'm reminded how grateful I was to a Wal-Mart clerk. Just days after surgery I had to appear in court for my divorce hearing. My knee was still very bandaged and the only thing I could get over it was sweatpants or yoga pants. I decided I felt well enough that day to drive into Wal-Mart for a cheap skirt to wear. No big deal, right?

I forgot to factor in it was the weekend before Thanksgiving. I forgot to factor in how crowded it got with the after-church group and how nervous I would be about getting knocked off my crutches. I forgot to consider how warm I would be in sweatpants and a long sleeve sweatshirt inside the store with the heat on during an unusually warm day.

As I hobbled through the aisles of Wal-Mart there wasn't a skirt in sight. I shouldn't have driven here so I surely can't leave and drive even farther to another store. I'm hot. It's crowded. I'm in pain. How can there be no skirts for sale here?

My mental stability quickly eroded away in the Wal-Mart Ladies section!

Eventually a saleswoman saw me, assessed my teary eyes and red face and offered to help me. As I stood in one spot crying and shaking, she ran through the aisles trying to find a skirt. Finally she found a pretty flowing black skirt, but it was from the plus section and entirely too big for me.

That's it. I'd officially lost it. I didn't want to be on crutches. I didn't want to be in pain. I really didn't want to be shopping for clothes in Wal-Mart to wear to a hearing for a divorce I never wanted!

The very nice saleslady found the smallest plus size skirt she could and helped me over to the fitting room. With some creative pinning she assured us both that the skirt wouldn't fall off me as I walked (hobbled) through the court room.

She was right. The skirt stayed on and I held my head high as I placed my crutches one step at a time in front of the judge.

Even in a large chain discount store gratitude is possible.

Gratitude is always possible. And on days I struggle to find gratitude, I remind myself that I am blessed and grateful that all my problems are first world problems.

Find Your Happy Place

At the time we bought our house in Tennessee, my children were all still quite young and I was still quite a mess. I decided

I needed a place to call my own, to go to when I needed a break. I needed a serenity spot.

So one weekend my husband and I began pulling up bushes, digging dirt and landscaping the front of the house. The serenity spot was my vision and I was adamant about where I wanted rocks placed, flowers planted and I insisted on a water fountain in the corner. My husband was basically just there to do the heavy work and he did it without complaining.

Finally after a couple days in the hot sun, my serenity spot was complete. I had found the perfect porch swing on sale and as I placed the cushions on the swing I stepped back and for the first time in a very long time felt a bit of contentment.

This was mine. My escape. My serenity spot.

But while I was out running errands that evening, my husband and his friend decided it would be funny to play a joke on me. So as I pulled into the driveway that night, I'm sure with visions of my serenity spot waiting for me, I found my husband and his friend sitting on my swing with beer cans and trash thrown all throughout the ground and gardens.

I was hurt. I stood stoic but inside my soul was crying. I don't remember what I said, if I said anything. But I do remember thinking, 'You will not take this from me.'

In hindsight I'm pretty sure my husband meant no ill intent that night. I know after all the back-breaking work he thought it was a bit of comic relief. I took his joke as a personal dig on my need for space. Was it insensitive? Yes. Was I ultra-sensitive? Yes. The spot was quickly cleaned up and restored.

But this many years later I remember the hurt. I've chosen to move past the hurt and enjoy my space.

Over the years my serenity spot has been the place I've read books, catnapped in the afternoon sun and sat and looked at the moon. It's also become the place for my teen boys to sit with their girlfriends, my middle son to listen to his favorite podcasts and the home base for the younger kids games of tag. It was the only place I found peace on those horrible nights of insomnia during the early days of my divorce.

Remember earlier when I told you about the night I sat in the closet crying and trying to pry open the gun safe with a screw-driver? My outside serenity spot is where I went that horrible night to calm down. Having that place to go to saved my life during the worst of my depression. I slept outside on that swing many nights with the dog at my side standing guard.

Now, in the evenings the kids will often sit on the swing and talk to me while I water the flower gardens. More often though I'll wait until after dark when the kids are already settled to go outside and water. I know watering the flowers could be seen as a chore. But to me, it's one of my happy places. Standing there with the hose or pulling weeds is a form of meditation for me. The sound of the water hitting the leaves, the smell of the mint as the water hits the herbs, even the frog that almost every night shows up to jump through the garden while I water bring me to a place of awareness that I can let go of the days stresses, be grateful for what I have, and realize that I am a part of something bigger.

Find your happy place. Stake out a small corner someplace and make it your serenity spot. Maybe place a scented candle, a favorite picture, Bible or prayer beads in that place. Let this be the one spot that you don't allow to become cluttered or abused.

The corner of my bedroom used to be the go-to throw it spot for anything I didn't know what else to do with. Laundry, bags of clothes waiting for the donation bin, even me and the girls Hula Hoops found their way here. My bedroom felt cluttered and seeing all the extra stuff laying around just added to my too-much-to-do stress level.

Then one of my clients asked if I wanted a recliner chair she was getting rid of. My original plan was to put it in the living room, but then I realized my bedroom corner was where it belonged. I spent an hour or so rearranging the bedroom, finally clearing away the clutter and the chair fit perfectly! And, even better, I finally knew what to do with my mom's prayer shawl that had been stuffed in the back of my closet. As I draped the shawl over the chair I once again stepped back and felt contentment. I felt at peace.

At night after my mom duties are complete, I can sit in the chair to read, write or even watch television. I've got a reminder of my mom with me. The chair is my inside serenity spot.

Military families often have a "love me wall" in their home. It's a place for the military person to hang up his awards and achievements. After years of looking at my husband's love me wall, I decided it was time for my own.

My wall has a picture of me riding horses on the beach in Mexico, the ticket from the time my mom and I saw the Dalai Lama, and assorted artwork and pictures I've created. As I spend time in my inside serenity spot, I can look to the wall next to me and see pictures of my travels and my accomplishments. It's a reminder that I am more than just an over-tired working single mom. I'm also a woman who loves life and embraces opportunities.

Tips for creating your own serenity space:

- First look at where you feel happy and content. Start there.
- Clear the area of clutter and distraction.

- Make the area pleasing to your senses; candles, pictures, flowers, pillows, etc.

- The space should be a place to heal yourself from the battles of the day. Therefore don't bring in work from the office, chores, or anything you feel you have to do. Only allow in what you want and what calms you.

- A soothing Epsom salt bath in the evening is very calming. Put the kids bath toys out of sight for just a little while and make the space your own personal spa.

- Most of us have limited space, so don't get caught up in making your serenity space an actual physical place. I've found my happy place in my evening walks, sitting outside to look at the moon and walking along a park path.

- Others make their happy place organizing scrapbooks, tending a garden, walking the dog, cooking, quilting or simply sitting outside at the end of a long day.

Every yoga class ends with savasana, or final relaxation. It's a time for the body to rest after the physical workout and a time for the mind to rest amidst the days list of responsibilities. New yogi's often fidget, squirm or even get up and leave during savasana. But final relaxation is the most important part of your yoga class.

I'm very laid back with my classes as to what pose they choose for savasana. Some students prefer viparita karani (legs up the wall), some lay flat on their yoga mats, other students curl up with a blanket. Any position that you give yourself permission to relax is fine. I tell my students whatever responsibilities the day has laid out for them will be waiting when they are done.

They aren't missing anything. A few of my long-time students now call savasana their happy place.

Our bodies need rest. Our minds need downtime. Our souls need a safe place to simply breathe and be.

"Tension is who you think you should be. Relaxation is who you are."

-- Chinese proverb

Mudita

People who are unhappy work very hard at making those around them unhappy as well. They begrudge the success of others and feel that the world is out to get them.

Happy people want others to be happy and see the world as one of abundant opportunity for everyone. Happy people experience mudita – appreciative and vicarious joy.

The root of the Sanskrit word mudita means to have a sense of gladness. Patanjali described mudita as to be delighted. As I was scrolling through my emails one night, I found one from a sender I didn't recognize yet the subject line quickly caught my attention. Amma The Hugging Saint, a Hindu spiritual leader and humanitarian, was going to visit and offer public blessings in Nashville, just three hours away from me. I decided this email was a sign I was supposed to completely rearrange my schedule and make the six hour round trip to receive a blessing that was taking place less than a week away.

Except the Universe didn't cooperate in rearranging my schedule. The kids had a summer schedule I'd worked hard and spent money to arrange, I had yoga clients expecting me, and the six hour trip would realistically be an overnight trip considering how many visitors usually show up to wait for a chance to meet Amma. My blessing wasn't going to happen.

As I shared my disappointment after class one night, one of my students, Amy, asked who Amma was. I explained, and then we both quickly realized that Amy was going to be in Nashville at the same time as Amma.

Amy has been a yoga student of mine for about six years now and has made amazing progress. Twenty years ago she was in a car accident and suffered severe brain trauma. She was now preparing to travel to Nashville to meet with a top neurosurgeon to discuss whether she was a candidate for a delicate brain surgery to reduce her tremors.

The Universe's plan was suddenly clear. The email may have come to my inbox, but it wasn't meant for me.

As Amy left for Nashville it was unclear if she would have time between all her doctor appointments to try and meet Amma. I told her if it was meant to be it would happen.

Two days later I got this text:

"Just saw Amma! And was blessed! Amazing experience!"

I texted back one word, "Mudita."

Even though I couldn't be there, I was genuinely happy for my friend. I could see the smile behind her text and it made me smile and filled me with joy. Her happiness is my happiness.

Mudita is the ability to show joy and celebrate the happi ess and achievements of others even if the daily details of our own lives are less than joyous. The Dalai Lama teaches that your happiness is just as important as the happiness of all the other billions of people in the world. If you can be happy when good things happen to others, your opportunities to be happy are increased exponentially!

Often the biggest obstacle to our ability to experience mudita is our own harsh criticism of ourselves. Most women are their own worst critic and are quick to tell themselves they don't deserve success. When we judge and compare our life to those around us, we isolate ourselves. We begin to feel we are deficient and unworthy. Then resentment kicks in and we find reasons that the other person is unworthy as well. It's a vicious cycle that only goes downward.

Mudita stops that cycle in its tracks. Living from a belief of unlimited abundance means there is enough success for you, for me, and for my friend. Love, joy and happiness aren't finite concepts. Just as a mother's heart grows bigger to allow room to love each new child she gives birth to, there is an abundance of joy available in the world. Happiness connects us all together to support, uplift and feel genuine joy for each other.

Laugh At Your Fears

Knowing that my mom's time on earth was coming to an end, my six kids and myself boarded a plane late on Christmas Eve night to fly home before a massive blizzard blanketed the entire northeastern United States and closed down the roads and airports. We were literally in a race against the weather, and against time, to get home to my mom.

It was our last chance to all be together and nothing was going to stop me from getting there. We were nine people sharing a two-bedroom, one-bathroom house with daily visits from the hospice nurses. Although we tried to maintain happy faces, the stress and fear of the inevitable were getting to all of us.

What had started out as a disagreement between me and Kid 2 over a purchase at the mall had quickly escalated into an all-out fight over anything and everything else. Neither one of us was about to back down. And neither one of us was able to admit we really weren't angry, we were sad and scared that my mom, their grandmother, was about to die.

The argument had been going on long enough that the rest of the kids were now upset and more than a couple of us had started crying. Finally my son stood up, pointed his finger at me and said "You haven't done yoga for ten days. You have a dark soul!"

Now to truly appreciate the magnitude of what he said, you need to use your best Darth Vader voice and re-read that line.

"You have a dark soul!"

As he finished his proclamation on the state of my soul, a blanket of silence fell upon the room. We just stood there looking at each other's tear-stained faces, stunned into silence.

And then we burst out laughing. And together we laughed and cried and laughed some more. Why were we arguing over petty matters now? We were wasting precious time that we could never get back.

Lying upstairs in her hospital bed, my mom awoke to the sound of our laughter. As I explained what was so funny, she began both laughing and crying too. I tried to apologize for the argument waking her up, but she couldn't hear me. She was laughing too hard over the dark soul comment. When we finally got ourselves under control, she looked at me and said, "Its Okay. I'm not afraid to die."

Living in the absence of fear allows you to live in a state of joy. You will never find contentment if you are afraid of what may happen or what someone else might do.

The world is as it is. You can't control it. But when you are happy, the world is a different place.

When you are ready to let go of the picture of how you think your life is supposed to be, you will be ready to let yourself enjoy your life as it is. The only guarantee we really have is that change is inevitable. The world, and your life, are in a constant state of flux. The more we try to bend the world to our control, the stronger we hold on, the less content and more stressed we become.

Knowing when to let go is probably one of the bravest most beneficial practices you will ever do for yourself.

Laughter, Love, and Letting Go*

"When the heart weeps for what it has lost, the soul laughs

for what it has found."

--- Suphi aphorism

Before my mom died, we had many talks about her final wishes and she was adamant she didn't want to be buried or have a final resting place where my sister and I would feel obligated to visit her. She decided on cremation, but again with the condition we spread her ashes somewhere nice and not leave them in an urn in our home.

So after her funeral I carried her box of ashes through airport security and once home I promptly put her up on the shelf in the back of my closet until I could figure out a more fitting place.

Months passed. Months of one injury and illness after another for me. Months of not weeping over my loss, but anger at my mom for leaving me, the doctors for not curing her, cancer for killing her and even God for taking her. I spent a lot of time confused and upset because I hadn't heard from her since her passing. Before she left I made her promise to come visit me.

But there was nothing. No visits. No odd feelings of her presence. No levitating dishes or items in the house mysteriously moved. I was frustrated and annoyed and stuck.

Now before I continue with this story I need to tell you my mom was an animal lover. Yes, we all love our animals. But my mom treated her dogs exceptionally well. In fact I often joked that after my death I wanted to return as one of my moms dogs because I knew I'd have a pretty cushy life. She loved her dogs to the point we even sneaked her dog in to the hospice center to visit her. Right before Mom got sick my family got a new puppy and mom mentioned many times how sad she was she'd never get to meet the new dog.

Her ashes continued to sit in my closet. One beautiful fall Saturday morning, I woke up and decided Mom should be placed in my front garden under the new mums I was planting. I pulled weeds, dug in the dirt, planted bulbs and made ready this garden that would be a tribute to my mom. I turned to Kid 2 and asked him to open the cremation box so I could pour some of her ashes in the dirt.

He opened the box, the bag got stuck, and my beloved mothers ashes fell out all over his pants, his shoes and into a pile on the ground.

We stood there for a brief moment not knowing what to do. Finally my son shouted “Get her off of me!”

Before I even had a chance to think about how to get my mom’s ashes off my son’s clothes, we were interrupted by new puppy who ran up, stuck her nose in the ashes, and immediately began rolling around in them.

My beloved mother’s ashes are now on my son’s sneakers and in my dogs fur!

All we could do was laugh. And laugh some more. And cry. And laugh some more. This is what Mom would have wanted. This chaos of kids and dogs and dirt. She wouldn’t have wanted ceremony and sadness. She would have wanted laughter and tears.

As I scooped up as much of the ashes as I could off my kid’s pants, as I brushed out the dog while standing in the garden, I decided it is done. Her physical state is gone. But her spirit lives on in my garden, in my laughter and in my dogs fur.

*Originially published Elephant Journal Decemeber 3, 2011

Don't wait to look back and laugh when something becomes funny. If it will be funny in ten years or ten minutes from now, laugh now! I know people who need more pomp and circumstance than I do might read the story of the dog rolling in my mom's ashes and think its disrespectful. Oh come on, it's funny!

I had a choice, I could cry and be upset that the ashes didn't get spread as I thought they should get spread, or I could laugh and take pleasure in the fact that it was never really in my control anyway.

Laughter and crying are similar emotions in that they both help us express the powerful feelings we are having at that moment. It usually takes an extreme event to trigger either laughter or tears. And they both usually occur when we feel vulnerable. Have you ever looked at someone and not known if they were laughing or crying? Heavy laughter and deep crying can even look and sound alike.

It's okay to laugh. It's okay to cry. Go ahead. Allow yourself to be vulnerable and emotional.

Sat Chit Ananda

I get it. Really I do. You're tired. You're struggling. You're tired of struggling. When you are in the throes of chaos it's so much easier to react in anger, sadness or depression. And all this talk of happiness and love sounds like a bunch of nonsense.

If your life is in chaos right now there are days you probably walk around feeling like nothing more than a swirling cloud of black energy. It would be easy to suc cumb and feed the blackness with sugar, fat and negativity.

You've become comfortable in your habits and familiar with your routine. Even if it's an unhappy daily routine, it's familiar and feels safe. Stepping out is scary. You think maybe its better to stay here than take a chance and reach for change.

But is this the life you want? Is this the life your soul is craving?

When you want to be happy, when you believe it will kill you to spend another day in misery, you will then be ready to turn your face to the sun and choose joy.

One of the first mantras I learned when beginning my yoga practice was the sat chit ananda mantra. Back then I thought mantras were a little too woo woo for me. But really I just didn't understand them. A mantra is nothing more than a mind tool. Personal affirmations, positive thinking and mantras help us stand strong when outside influences try and beat us down. Translated, the sat chit ananda mantra means:

Sat – truth, free yourself from limitations

Chit – knowledge, only in a state of awakening can you truly experience life

Ananda – bliss

Once you are willing to speak the truth you will become aware and awake to what you really desire and joy will follow.

If a Sanskrit mantra is too woo woo for you to repeat right now try the more familiar peace, love, joy. Every day, strive for peace, strive for love, strive for joy.

Stand strong, speak the truth, stay aware and open your arms to the joyful life that awaits you. Namaste.

"When you realize how PERFECT everything is... you will tilt your head back and laugh at the sky."

Buddha

VIKRAM

Make a gratitude list. List five things daily that you are grateful for. They don't have to be major accomplishments. Find gratitude and joy in the little things!

Laugh every day!

Turn your face to the sun and enjoy the warmth.

Create a serenity spot.

Find your happy place and be intentional about going there regularly.

Make it your intention to be social. Smile at a stranger in the grocery store, the mall, the post office, etc.

Make a choice to always choose joy.

Get outside in nature. Turn off the phone and just become present in your surroundings.

When faced with a difficult situation, make it your habit to stop and first take a deep breath. Rather than reacting out of fear or anger, address the situation from a place of love and compassion.

GRATITUDE LIST

Make a go-to gratitude list right here for those days when you are struggling to find anything to be grateful for. There is no wrong reason to be grateful. Write anything that makes you smile.

MEDITATION MOMENT

Find a quiet, comfortable place to sit. Preferably somewhere that you will feel or at least see the sun. Turn your body and your face upward to the sun.

Make any adjustments you need to make to allow your body to be comfortable and relaxed. Bring your hands to your lap, your right hand open and resting in the palm of your left hand. Relax your shoulders. Find your breath.

Begin your even count breathing. Inhale for about three slow counts, exhale for the same three slow counts. There is no magic number here. If you can inhale and exhale deeper, please do so.

Once you've found a smooth even pattern to your breath, imagine a smile spreading over your face. You won't actually move any facial muscles. Just allow the feeling of a smile to envelop over you.

Allow the external warmth of the sun to merge with the internal serenity you feel inside. Allow the peace to spread from the bottom of your toes, up your legs and through your hips. Feel the warmth rise up along your torso, out to your arms and fingers and over your shoulders. Notice how much lighter your neck and your head feel.

Imagine this peaceful feeling as a white light spreading through and radiating out from your body. You are the embodiment of peace. Your presence emits love. You create joy.

Stay here as long as is comfortable or as long as life allows. When ready, bring your hands together in front of your heart with thumbs touching your breastbone. Take one final deep, slow breath and on the exhale bow your head.

Namaste

AFFIRMATION

I am thankful for both the beauty and the grace in my life. I am surrounded by joy and abundance. My life is perfect exactly as it is.

I am at peace.

Mom's Fudge Recipe

4 cups sugar

1 can evaporated milk

1 stick butter

1 12oz bag chocolate chips

1 8oz jar peanut butter (chunky peanut butter is nice)

1 8oz jar marshmallow cream

1 teaspoon vanilla

In large pot bring sugar, evaporated milk, and butter to a boil. Continue boiling nine minutes or sugar mixture reaches 180 degrees.

Remove from heat and add chocolate chips, peanut butter, marshmallow cream and vanilla.

Stir until thoroughly blended, pour into flat pan with edges.

Allow to cool completely.

Eat and enjoy!

EPILOGUE

July 2014: I'm sitting alone in an emergency room, terrified and in shock. Kid 1 is behind those doors, and because he is now technically an adult, I'm not allowed back there next to him.

Dear God I'll make any bargain, any deal you ask. Just please let him be okay.

I've been through so much I don't know how much more I can take. When will it end?

As I drove to the hospital way too fast on a stormy night over wet roads I made only two calls. At the time, I had little information to give. My calls were mostly to make sure someone would check in on the other kids who were left home as I screeched out of my driveway.

As I sat alone that night my brain played out every worst-case scenario possible. Soon I was convinced this was how my story ended. I can handle anything, but not the loss of one of my children. I can't do this anymore.

As the storm raged on outside I looked up as the doors opened and in walked one of my closest friends. She had been one of the calls I made and she, too, drove too fast over wet roads to sit with me all night in the emergency room.

'We're not in the morgue", she kept telling me. "We're not in the morgue. So we're going to get through this."

She kept using that word. We.

The weeks after were spent learning to deal with a new reality. I had to rely on my strength, yes, but I also had to rely on others. This wasn't something I was going to be able to control and solve on my own. I had no choice but to ask for help from the professionals and from my friends.

I finally knew better than to try and handle everything alone. I was very careful with whom I chose to share this latest crisis. But I didn't feel the need to take on the burden of it being a secret.

It took a crisis with one of my children for me to finally lay down my need to control and to give up my need to prove I don't need help. I can't control everything and I do need help. As a mom I'll do anything to save my kids and protect my family.

Asking for help isn't a reflection of my weakness. Accepting the generosity of my friends doesn't mean I'm failing to provide myself. It means I am wise enough to know that not only can't I do this alone, but that I don't need to do it alone.

I am not alone.

Namaste

I honor the place in you

In which the entire universe dwells.

I honor the place in you

Which is of love, of truth,

Of light, and of peace.

When you are in that place in you

And I am in that place in me,

We are one.

November 2005

My life is in chaos but I have no choice

to put on a happy face.

October 2011

We are all getting older but I'm beginning to find myself. Smiling because I have no idea what is about to happen to my life.

April 2015

The night we tried to take this picture ended with two kids fighting and one very frustrated mom. We are too big to all fit on the bed, the kids are too busy with their own lives to sit still long enough for a group picture, and it was too late at night to even be attempting this.

But I'm leaving the picture here because, for better or worse, we are a family.

We laugh.

We fight.

We love.

October 2014

For some reason I have very few pictures of me and my mom together. As a teen I hated how similar we were. Now, I am proud to say I am just like my mom.

FURTHER READING

These are just a few books that have impacted me over the years and I hope they will offer some guidance to you as well. This is by no means a complete list and I encourage you to seek out other references and guide books as you take your own journey.

Growing The Positive Mind ~ by Dr. William K. Larkin

Something More: Excavating Your Authentic Self ~ By Sarah Ban Breathnach

Happy Yoga ~ By Steve Ross

Natural Prozac: Learning to Release Your Body's Own Anti-Depressants ~ By Joel Robertson

Opening Our Hearts Transforming Our Losses ~ Al-Anon Family Groups

Buddha A Story of Enlightenment ~ By Deepak Chopra

Learning to Breathe My Yearlong Quest to Bring Calm to My

Life ~ By Priscilla Warner

The Woman's Book of Yoga & Health ~ By Linda Sparrowe

Eating Mindfully ~ By Susan Albers

One Day At A Time in Al-Anon ~ By Al-Anon Family Groups

The Alchemist ~ By Paulo Coelho

The Essential Rumi ~ Translated By Coleman Barks

Courage To Change: One Day At A Time in Al-Anon II ~ By Al-Anon Family Groups

ABOUT THE AUTHOR

Jennifer Williams-Fields is passionate about writing, yoga, traveling and being a fabulous single momma to six super kids. Doing it all at one time, however, is her great struggle. She has been teaching yoga since 2005 and writing since she first picked up a crayon. Although her life is a sort of organized chaos, she loves every minute of the chaos and is grateful for all she's learned along the way. Jennifer has written for various magazines and newspapers, is the co-author of "HELP! 9 Solutions for a F'd Up Life". She is a contributing writer for Rebelle Society, YourTango, YogaUOnline.com and Elephant Journal at http://www.elephantjournal.com/author/jennifer-fields/

Follow Jennifer on Twitter @yogalifeway, Instagram @ JNELF6 and read her YogaLifeWay blog; A Yogi's Journey Through Diapers, Detentions and Downdogs.

Made in the USA
Lexington, KY
15 June 2015